A FIELD GUIDE TO
REPTILES AND AMPHIBIANS
OF TEXAS

A FIELD GUIDE TO
REPTILES AND AMPHIBIANS
OF TEXAS

BY JUDITH M. GARRETT AND DAVID G. BARKER
MAPS BY TERRY L. HIBBITTS

Gulf Publishing Company
Houston, Texas

Gulf Publishing Company
Book Division
P.O. Box 2608, Houston, Texas 77252-2608

10 9 8 7 6 5 4

Texas Monthly is a registered trademark of Mediatex Communications Corp.

Library of Congress Cataloging-in-Publication Data

Garrett, Judith M., 1944–
    A field guide to reptiles and amphibians of Texas / by Judith
M. Garrett and David G. Barker ; maps by Terry L. Hibbitts.
        p.   cm. — (Texas Monthly fieldguide series)
        Originally published: Austin, Tex. : Texas Monthly Press, c1987.
        Includes bibliographical references (p.   ) and index.
        ISBN 0-87719-091-7
        1. Reptiles—Texas—Identification. 2. Amphibians—Texas—
Identification. I. Barker, David G., 1952–   . II. Title. III. Title:
Reptiles and amphibians of Texas. IV. Series: Texas Monthly field
guide series.
        [QL653.T4G37   1994]
        597.6'09764—dc20   93-36731
                                                                                    CIP

Printed in Hong Kong.

Contents

TOADS AND FROGS
Toads: Family Bufonidae

Treefrogs and Relatives: Family Hylidae

Tropical Frogs: Family Leptodactylidae

Narrowmouth Toads: Family Microhylidae

Spadefoot Toads: Family Pelobatidae

True Frogs: Family Ranidae

Mexican Burrowing Toad: Family Rhinophrynidae

SALAMANDERS
Mole Salamanders: Family Ambystomatidae

Amphiumas: Family Amphiumidae

Mudpuppies: Family Proteidae

Lungless Salamanders: Family Plethodontidae

Newts: Family Salamandridae

Sirens: Family Sirenidae

Reptiles: Description of Orders

TURTLES
Marine Turtles: Family Cheloniidae

Snapping Turtles: Family Chelydridae

Leatherback Turtles: Family Dermochelyidae

Water Turtles and Box Turtles: Family Emydidae

Mud and Musk Turtles: Family Kinosternidae

Skinks: Family Scincidae

Whiptails: Family Teiidae

Acknowledgments

For assistance in the preparation of the manuscript for this field guide, special thanks must go to Terry L. Hibbitts who prepared the range maps, provided some of the photographs, spent many hours in the field looking for specimens on our behalf, and with great good humor encouraged our efforts in many ways.

We particularly wish to acknowledge and thank the Department of Biology of the University of Texas at Arlington and Edmund D. Brodie, chairman, for assistance and support.

Jonathan A. Campbell and William W. Lamar were constant sources of sound advice and friendly encouragement throughout the project; they read the manuscript and provided corrections and helpful comments. James R. Dixon graciously answered questions and provided information on several occasions.

Peggy Toal Garrett helped in the preparation of the glossary; and both she and Sharron Schumann assisted in other tedious details necessary to complete the manuscript. John L. Darling assisted with our work in the Museum of Herpetology at UTA. James B. Murphy provided reference works from his personal library.

We want to thank the following institutions for letting us photograph animals in their collections: the Caldwell Zoo, Tyler, TX; the Fort Worth Zoo, Fort Worth, TX; the Gladys Porter Zoo, Brownsville, TX; and the Chihuahua Desert Research Institute, Alpine, TX.

Photographers whose contributions helped complete the illustrations include the following: William W. Lamar, David W. Mabie, R. Andrew Odum, Peter C. H. Pritchard, David T. Roberts, Samuel S. Sweet, and Terry L. Vandeventer.

Countless hours of field collecting were contributed by the following: Donal Boyer, Pat Bradley, Mark Burleson, Jonathan Campbell, Jack Cover, Jimmy Forester, Rick Green, Toby Hibbitts, John Hunter, James Johnson, Bill Lamar, Steve Levey, Bob Maccon, Ken Magnuson, John McCord, Hugh McCrystal, Doug Mehaffey, Mark Nelson, Dave Roberts, Brad Shipman, Diane Shipman, Dude Sproul and his granddaughter Kerith Johnson and her friend Max.

As we traveled around the state collecting information, animals and photographs, we were seldom without a place to stay. We are grateful to the following people for their generous hospitality: Julian and Peggy Garrett, Zeke and Jeri Garrett, Barbara and Rayburn Houston, Bill and Nancy Lamar, Hugh McCrystal, Dude and Inell Sproul, and Dexter and Joni Tooke.

Introduction

Most of us have experienced the phenomenon of learning a new word and then running into it everywhere, as though the word itself had just come into the language. What has really happened, in most cases, is that the word was there all along, but not knowing its meaning, the reader did not notice it until new knowledge made it visible.

The same phenomenon applies to the animals that are all around us, even in urban environments, where the idea of wild animals seems to apply only to the zoo, not to our back yards. We don't see them, and yet, the animals are there. Every part of Texas is populated with a great diversity of animal life. With more knowledge of the animals around us, we are more likely to be aware of their presence.

Another hindrance to our awareness of the animals around us often lies in a too narrow definition of the words "wild animals." For many of us, wild animals are fur-bearing creatures rarely seen even in areas remote from our homes. And in our narrow-mindedness we overlook many of Texas' most interesting and beautiful animals.

The purpose of this guide is to assist readers in identifying animals they see and to inform them of others they may encounter here in Texas, even in their own back yards. Another aim is to provide readily accessible information about animals beyond the mammals: the frogs and toads, the lizards and skinks, the salamanders, the crocodilian, and the turtles that make Texas one of the richest of all the states in wildlife.

One hundred and sixty-seven Texas reptiles and amphibians are described in this field guide. Each animal is described in a separate entry, even when subspecies are very similar to each other, so that the reader can turn right to the entry in question for full information, without having to refer to other entries.

The descriptive language used includes some scientific terms, which are defined in a glossary, but the entries are written to be understood by the wide audience of nonscientists who nevertheless want accurate, detailed descriptions. The details of description focus on easily observed characteristics, or field marks, most of which can be seen without capturing the animal.

The entries are arranged alphabetically, first by class, then within each class by order, within each order by family, within each family by genus, within each genus by species, and finally by subspecies. All entries are indexed by family, common name, and scientific name, and the index includes the page numbers of the entries and photographs (bold-faced numbers indicate photographs).

1

Range maps included with each entry give a general idea of the animal's locale. The range of each animal is also described in the narrative of the entries.

The photographs were made, whenever possible, in the animal's natural environment. The others were made in recreated environments similar to the natural habitat of the animal. The photographs are of specimens found in Texas in every case possible. Some, however, were found in another state within the species' range. An appendix lists the location in which each specimen photographed was found.

Amphibians
Order Anura: Toads and Frogs

There are 46 toads and frogs in Texas, divided into 7 families: family Bufonidae, toads; family Hylidae, treefrogs and relatives; family Leptodactylidae, tropical frogs; family Microhylidae, narrowmouth toads; family Pelobatidae, spadefoot toads; family Ranidae, true frogs; and family Rhinophrynidae, represented by the Mexican burrowing toad.

Although there are no scientific rules to distinguish between toads and frogs, typically toads have warty skin and short legs, and frogs have smooth skin and long legs. Toads hop and frogs leap. All have well-developed forelegs and larger hind legs. They do not have well-defined necks. Each species and subspecies has a distinctive voice, and all have acute hearing, with well-developed ears and a conspicuous tympanum on both sides of the head.

Most lay their eggs in water, and most hatch into tadpoles, which later transform into frogs or toads. Individual entries cite any differences in reproductive behavior. All are carnivorous as adults and may be cannibalistic as tadpoles.

Toads and frogs are most easily observed at night with a flashlight after locating them by the sound of their calls.

Order Caudata: Salamanders

There are 24 salamanders in Texas, divided into 6 families: family Ambystomatidae, mole salamanders; family Amphiumidae, amphiumas; family Proteidae, mudpuppies; family Plethodontidae, lungless salamanders; family Salamandridae, newts; and family Sirenidae, sirens.

With their long bodies and tails and equal-sized forelegs and hind legs, many salamanders could be mistaken for lizards, but salamanders have smooth or warty skin, instead of scales, and they have no claws on their feet. Sirens and amphiumas are often mistaken for eels, but careful examination will reveal their small legs and feet, appendages never present in eels.

All must have abundant moisture in their habitats, and all are carnivorous. Most are nocturnal and secretive in their habits. Most lay eggs in water, and their aquatic larvae have external gills that are later lost during the transformation to adults.

Since identification of similar animals sometimes depends on the number of riblike costal grooves, that count is included in most entries.

Dwarf American Toad

Bufo americanus charlesmithi

Description   2½ inches maximum length. This small, often reddish toad has a short, round body and short, broad head with a wide snout. Its eyes are prominent, and its large, oblong parotoid glands are usually separate from the cranial crests or connected by short spurs. Its legs are short and sturdy. General coloration varies from reddish to brown to olive with dark brown spots, each spot containing one wart, which may be brown, yellow, or reddish. It may have a light middorsal stripe. The dorsal surface may have small areas of lighter colors. The ventral surface is lighter and may have faint spots. The male has dark coloration on the throat.

Voice   The vocal sac on males is round when inflated, and the call is a pleasant, high-pitched sustained musical trill. A single call may last up to 30 seconds, with a trill rate of 30 to 40 per second. Calls can be heard day and night during the height of the breeding season.

Range   This toad is widespread in the northeastern part of the United States, but in Texas it is found in only a small area along the Red River near the center of the Oklahoma border.

Habitat   Found in a variety of habitats, from suburban gardens to cultivated fields and river bottoms. It must have access to moist areas for shelter, pools for breeding, and an abundant supply of insects and other invertebrates for food.

Behavior   This mainly nocturnal toad eats insects and other invertebrates in great quantities. It shelters itself from heat under rocks and logs and in cold weather digs backward into moist soil to hibernate.

Reproduction   Breeding occurs from March to July, and eggs are laid in strings that attach to vegetation in pools. Eggs hatch in 3 to 12 days, and tadpoles transform between June and August, when they reach ¼ to ½ inch long.

Great Plains Toad

Bufo cognatus

Description 1⅞ to 4½ inches. This large, broad-bodied toad is gray to olive to brown and is distinguished by its large dark blotches with light-rimmed edges, which occur in symmetrical pairs on its back. Its head is broad, and its short snout has a conspicuous boss formed by prominent cranial crests that converge diagonally from the back of its head. It has elongated parotoid glands behind the cranial crests. Its hind legs are about the same length as the body, and each of the long hind feet has a sharp digging tubercle.

Voice The vocal sac is sausage-shaped when inflated and may be up to one third the size of the toad. When deflated the sac is concealed beneath a flap of light-colored skin on the throat. The call is a shrill metallic trill, which can be heard from great distances and which is deafening when heard in chorus at close range. Individual calls last 5 seconds to 1 minute, with a trill rate of 13 to 20 per second.

Range Found in northwestern parts of the state, north of a diagonal line drawn roughly from Wichita Falls to Presidio.

Habitat *B. cognatus* thrives in habitats that are drier than many other toads prefer. It can be seen in open grasslands, brushy areas, or cultivated fields where cutworms are present. It may also be found near irrigation ditches, in riverbeds and streambeds, and on floodplains. It prefers a habitat with soil loose enough for easy burrowing.

Behavior Primarily nocturnal, it may also be active on cloudy, rainy days. It consumes large quantities of cutworms and burrows easily in loose soil. When threatened, it may inflate its body, close its eyes, and lower its head to the ground, camouflaging itself with a rocklike or clodlike appearance.

Reproduction Breeding occurs from April to September, usually during or after rainfall. It lays single or double egg strings in pools of water, and they attach to vegetative debris. The prominent V-shaped cranial crest is evident even on very young toads.

Eastern Green Toad

Bufo debilis debilis

Description   1¼ to 2 inches. This small, bright green toad has many dark green to black spots on its back and legs, with warts on each spot. Its head and body appear flattened, and the head is narrow with widely spaced eyes and a pointed snout. It has large, distinctly separated parotoids, which may extend downward to the jaw. It has no cranial crests. Its legs are short, with the hind legs usually shorter than the overall length of the body. Male and female are similar, except that the male has a black or dusky throat. The undersides of both sexes are pale olive or nearly white.

Voice   When extended, the vocal sac is round and reaches the tip of the chin. The call is a sustained, shrill cricketlike trill lasting up to 7 seconds, at 5- or 6-second intervals. Males call while floating, with their heads held out of the water.

Range   This toad is found from Oklahoma to Mexico, through the central and west-central part of Texas, as well as in the eastern part of the Panhandle.

Habitat   Thriving in unusually dry habitats for toads, it is found on open, grassy plains near pools where breeding takes place.

Behavior   Primarily nocturnal, this toad is rarely seen except during and after heavy rains. It burrows under rocks and seeks temporary shelter under clumps of grass, from where males call during the breeding period. When threatened, it may flatten its body against the ground.

Reproduction   Breeding takes place from March to September when rain has sufficiently filled pools, ditches, or streambeds. If conditions are not favorable, it will not breed. Egg strings are attached to vegetation in the water. Tadpoles transform quickly, at ⅓ to ⅖ inch, because of the temporary nature of the breeding pools in their arid and semiarid habitats.

6

Western
Green
Toad

Bufo debilis insidior

Description 1¼ to 2⅛ inches. This small flat toad is usually a paler, sometimes more yellow-green color than the eastern green toad. It is covered with many small warts and black spots on its back and legs, and the spots are usually interconnected in a weblike pattern. Male and female are similar in coloration, except that the throat of the male is dark. Undersides are pale olive or nearly white. The toad has large oval parotoid glands that extend downward. It has no cranial crests. The head is narrow, and the prominent eyes are widely separated. Its legs are short, with the hind legs usually shorter than the length of the body.

Voice The vocal sac is round when extended, and the male may call while floating with his head out of the water. The call is a shrill, cricketlike trill lasting up to 7 seconds at intervals of 5 seconds or more.

Range Found in the western part of the Panhandle and in the far western triangle of the state.

Habitat Like the eastern green toad, it thrives in dry habitats. It is found on arid and semiarid plains and grasslands near pools and streambeds that fill during rains.

Behavior Primarily nocturnal, this toad is usually active only during or after heavy rains. It hides under rocks or clumps of grass. When threatened, it may flatten itself against the ground. It may call from its hiding place under a clump of grass.

Reproduction Breeding takes place from March to September, but only when rain fills pools or ditches where the toads spawn. If rains do not occur, it may skip breeding. Egg strings are attached to vegetation in pools, and tadpoles transform quickly, at ⅓ to ⅖ inch, because of the temporary nature of the breeding pools in their arid and semiarid habitats.

Houston Toad

Bufo houstonensis

Description   2 inches to a record 3¼ inches total length at rest. This medium-sized toad has prominent cranial crests that thicken particularly behind the eyes. Spurs on the outside edges of the cranial crests touch the elongated parotoids. General coloration is varied from light brown to gray or purplish gray, sometimes with patches of green. Dark mottling on the back may create vague zigzag lines, and there is often a light mid-dorsal line. Pale ventral surfaces often have small dark spots. Male and female are similar, except that the male has a dark throat.

Voice   The vocal sac on males is round when inflated, and the call is a sustained, high-pitched musical trill. A single call may last 4 to 11 seconds, with a trill rate of 32 per second.

Range   Found only in a rather small pocket of southeastern Texas, from Harris County to Bastrop County.

Habitat   Found in pine forests and prairies with sandy ridges.

Behavior   This mainly nocturnal toad eats a variety of insects and other invertebrates. Males call from or near pools rimmed with grass.

Reproduction   Breeding takes place from February to June, when rains create shallow pools. During years when rainfall permits, breeding may be repeated, occurring first in early spring and then again in early summer.

Giant Toad

Bufo marinus

Description 4 to 7 inches. This toad is aptly named, being the largest toad in the world. Females are larger than males, and both sexes have huge, deeply pitted triangular parotoid glands extending down the sides of the body. The overall body shape is round and flattened. The cranial crests are quite prominent. General coloration is variable, from shades of brown to yellow, red, or even olive-green. It may have a light middorsal stripe, and on either side of the midline there may be a row of large, fleshy warts running the length of the body. The rows of warts are more prominent on males.

Voice Males call with a round vocal sac in a slow, rhythmical, low-pitched trill that can be heard at great distance.

Range In Texas, this toad is found only in the southern part of the state along the Rio Grande, but not including the southeastern tip.

Habitat Found primarily in or near natural pools and arroyos, it may also appear in other humid environments, such as in gardens and near man-made ponds.

Behavior Primarily nocturnal, this toad feeds voraciously on beetles, cockroaches, and a variety of other insects and invertebrates, as well as on other amphibians and even reptiles. During the day it seeks shelter under stones, logs, or boards or in burrows that it digs in soft earth. It is particularly resistant to predation because when threatened it secretes a highly toxic and probably foul-tasting milky substance from its skin and glands. The secretion can cause skin and eye irritation in humans and can be lethal to an animal that bites the toad.

Reproduction Breeding takes place year-round, whenever rain and temperature are suitable. It lays eggs in strings in standing water, as well as in canals and streams. Hatching occurs in less than 3 days, and tadpoles transform after 45 days or less.

Red-spotted Toad
Bufo punctatus

Description 1½ to 3 inches. This small toad has a flattened body and round parotoid glands about the size of the eye. The snout is pointed and the head is quite flat, with only slightly developed cranial crests or none at all. The eyes are large and widely spaced. The dorsal surfaces may be light gray, olive, or reddish brown, usually with an even covering of small reddish warts. Some individuals are quite pale and unmarked with warts. Ventral surfaces are pale, usually dingy white or buff, and on the male the throat is dusky.

Voice The vocal sac is round, and the call is a pleasant birdlike trill, high-pitched and nearly constant for its 4- to 10-second duration. Males usually call from the water's edge, sitting on rocks or debris.

Range Found throughout the western half of the state and in west-central portions, but not including the Lower Rio Grande Valley.

Habitat This toad thrives in dry habitats, appearing in desert and open grassland, but it requires a constant source of moisture, such as desert oases, springs, seepages, pools along streams, and cattle tanks.

Behavior Chiefly nocturnal, this small toad is most active at twilight, and it may be diurnal during breeding. It climbs onto rocks with ease, and it may seek shelter in rock crevices. It may also enter mammal burrows. It feeds on a variety of insects.

Reproduction Breeding takes place from April to September when rains occur. It lays eggs singly in rock-bottomed pools. Eggs are protected by a sticky jelly and hatch in about 3 days. Tadpoles transform after 40 to 60 days.

Texas Toad

Bufo speciosus

Description 2 to 3⅝ inches maximum length. This round, plump toad has a short snout and is generally olive to grayish brown. It is uniformly covered with small warts and often has a random scattering of dark blotches on its back that surround greenish-brown warts. It has no middorsal stripe. It has indistinct cranial crests or none at all. The parotoid glands are oval-shaped and widely separated. Its only truly distinctive features are 2 sharp-edged tubercles on each hind foot. They are black, and the inner one on each foot is sickle-shaped.

Voice The vocal sac of this toad is oblong and about one third the size of the body when inflated. It is olive-colored, and when deflated it is covered by a fold of pale skin. The call is a series of abrupt high-pitched trills lasting only about ½ second, with a trill rate during that brief explosion of sound of 39 to 57 per second. The interval between trills is about 1 second.

Range Found throughout most of the state, except for the western Panhandle and East Texas.

Habitat Adapted to dry conditions, this toad prefers sandy soils and may be seen in a variety of habitats ranging from prairies to open woodlands to cultivated regions. Its sources of moisture in dry locales are cattle tanks, irrigation ditches, and temporary rain pools.

Behavior This nocturnal toad is a skilled burrower in loose soil. When threatened, if it is unable to burrow, it will flatten itself against the ground to avoid detection.

Reproduction Breeding takes place from April to September, but only after rains. It deposits eggs in still pools left from rains or in man-made water holes, such as ditches, cattle tanks, or reservoirs.

Gulf Coast Toad

Bufo valliceps valliceps

Description 2 to 5⅛ inches total length. This medium-sized, rather flat toad is distinctively marked by a broad dark stripe down each side, bordered above by a light stripe. It has a third light stripe down the middle of its back beginning on its head. General coloration varies from yellowish brown to almost black. On males the throat is yellowish green. Most individuals have a distinct narrow dark line running the length of the upper lip just above the pale lip area. The prominent cranial crests form a depression on top of the skull. The ridges of the crests may be dark. Triangular parotoid glands are connected to the cranial crest behind the eyes.

Voice The vocal sac on this toad is large and round when extended. The call is a short, flat trill of 2 to 6 seconds that is repeated often at intervals of 1 to 4 seconds.

Range Found in most of East Texas, except the northeastern corner, and throughout Central and South Texas.

Habitat This toad is at home in a variety of moist habitats, including man-made ditches, backyard gardens, dump sites, and storm sewers. It is also found on barrier beaches along the coast, as well as on coastal prairies.

Behavior Most active at twilight, this toad can be seen under streetlights at night or in other spots where it can feed on insects drawn to lights.

Reproduction Breeding takes place from March to September. It lays eggs in strings of jelly, usually in double rows. Tadpoles transform after 20 to 30 days.

East
Texas
Toad

Bufo velatus

Description 2 to 3 inches maximum length. The appearance of this toad varies widely in different locales. General coloration may be yellowish brown to brown, greenish brown, or nearly black. The paler chest has dark spots. The toad has a light mid-dorsal stripe and may have vague lateral light stripes. Cranial crests are prominent, and parotoid glands are elongated.

Voice The call of this toad also varies widely. It is similar to the calls of the Woodhouse's toads, which are likened to the bleating of a sheep. The call may be formed from repeated trills lasting 5 to 10 seconds, or it may be more like a whirring sound extending to a prolonged single, low-pitched droning note.

Range Found throughout East Texas and south along the coastal plains, but not extending into far South Texas.

Habitat This toad prefers sandy areas near marshes, irrigation ditches, or temporary rain pools. It may also be seen in backyard gardens.

Behavior Active at night, this toad is often seen under lights feeding on insects. It burrows in sandy soil or seeks shelter in vegetation.

Reproduction Breeding takes place from March to August. Egg strings are attached to vegetation in shallow water.

Southwestern Woodhouse's Toad

Bufo woodhouseii australis

Description   2½ to 5 inches total length. This toad varies in coloration from yellow to green to brown, with irregular dark spots on its back and well-developed dark markings on its sides and chest. Otherwise, ventral surfaces are pale yellow. Individuals of this subspecies vary widely, but most have a light mid-dorsal line that usually does not extend onto the snout. On the male the throat is dark. The toad has prominent cranial crests and elongated parotoid glands.

Voice   Males call while sitting in water, and the vocal sac is round. The call is a nasal bleating sound lasting 1 to 2½ seconds, often dropping sharply in pitch at the end. The sound is often compared to the bleating of a sheep.

Range   Found along the upper Rio Grande drainage through southwestern Texas, including Big Bend but not extending downriver from there.

Habitat   Preferring sandy areas, this toad occupies a variety of habitats, including canyons, river bottoms, desert streams, irrigated fields, and back yards.

Behavior   Primarily nocturnal, it can commonly be seen feeding on insects drawn to sources of light. It may occasionally be active during the day, but it usually hides in vegetation or in burrows.

Reproduction   Breeding occurs from March to August, and egg strings are attached to vegetation in shallow water.

Woodhouse's Toad
Bufo woodhouseii woodhouseii

Description 2¼ to 5 inches total length. This round toad is generally greenish brown to yellowish brown and covered with numerous small warts. On its back are scattered dark blotches surrounding brownish warts. The dark blotches extend on some individuals onto the sides and legs, as well. It has a narrow, light middorsal stripe beginning on its short snout. Its paler chest is unspotted. The cranial crests may be dark, and the narrow parotoids usually touch the crest behind the eye.

Voice The vocal sac is round when inflated, and the call is a low-pitched bleating lasting 1 to 2½ seconds. Males call from pools of still water.

Range Found throughout central and north-central Texas and the Panhandle.

Habitat It prefers sandy areas and is found in a variety of habitats where sufficient moisture is present, such as near irrigation ditches in cultivated areas, in canyons near streams, near temporary rain pools, or in urban back yards.

Behavior Primarily nocturnal, it may feed on insects attracted to sources of light. It seeks shelter in burrows or hides in vegetation.

Reproduction Breeding takes place from March to August, and egg strings are attached to vegetation in shallow, still water.

Blanchard's Cricket Frog

Acris crepitans blanchardi

Description ⅝ to 1½ inches total length. This small frog is generally light gray to greenish brown, with indistinct dark markings on its back and dark bands on its legs. Its skin is rougher than that of other cricket frogs. It has a ragged dark stripe on the rear of the thigh, a white line from the eye to the base of the foreleg, and a dark triangle on the head with the apex pointing backward. Some individuals may have red or green markings in the middle of the back. The throat of the male is dark and may have some yellow. The frog's snout is long and rounded, and the toes are slender and extensively webbed.

Voice The vocal sac is round, and the call is a succession of clicks sounding like river rocks being tapped together. The call rate starts at about 1 per second and gradually increases.

Range Found throughout the state except for far East Texas, the western Panhandle, and the extreme western tip.

Habitat This frog prefers ponds of shallow water with plenty of vegetation in the water, grass around the rim, and full sun most of the day. It may also live in slow-moving streams with sunny banks.

Behavior This diurnal frog spends most of its time on the ground hopping among the grass and other vegetation. It is active all year and is often found in groups. If disturbed, it will leap quickly out of reach or skitter over the water's surface.

Reproduction Breeding takes place from February through the summer, depending on temperatures, with choruses heard as late as October in its southern range.

Northern Cricket Frog

Acris crepitans crepitans

Description   ⅝ to 1⅜ inches total length. This small frog has relatively short legs, a small head, and slender, extensively webbed toes. General coloration of the rough skin is gray-brown with some green, yellow, red, or black. It has dark markings on its back, dark bands on its legs, and a prominent black stripe on the rear of the thigh. It has the cricket frog's characteristic dark triangle on top of the head, with the apex pointing backward, and it has a white line from the eye to the base of the foreleg. The throat of the male is dusky, and the ventral surfaces may be spotted.

Voice   The vocal sac is round, and the call is a series of clicks, about 1 per second at first, then gaining speed. The sound is similar to that made by two stones being struck together.

Range   Found in the extreme eastern part of the state, in a narrow band from Arkansas to the Gulf of Mexico.

Habitat   This frog prefers shallow ponds with ample vegetation, both in and surrounding the water, and full sun during most of the day. It may also be seen in slow-moving streams with sunny banks.

Behavior   This diurnal frog basks in the sun on the banks of ponds and streams and hops in the surrounding vegetation to evade detection. It may be seen basking in groups, and if threatened, it will leap high and quickly, even skittering over the surface of the water to avoid capture. It is active year-round.

Reproduction   Breeding takes place from February through the summer months, with choruses as late as October in its southern range.

Coastal Cricket Frog

Acris crepitans paludicola

Description ¾ to 1 inch total length. This small frog has smoother skin than other cricket frogs and little or no pattern on its back. The back is dark gray, and the legs are gray with dark bars. The belly and throat are pink, with deeper pigment on the throat. The snout is long and somewhat pointed, with prominent nostrils. The frog has relatively short legs and extensively webbed toes with prominent toe pads.

Voice The vocal sac is round and distinctly pink, and the call is a succession of clicks sounding like river rocks being tapped together. The call rate is about 1 per second and gradually increases.

Range Found along the eastern coast from Brazoria County to the Louisiana border.

Habitat This frog is at home in shallow pools of fresh or brackish water in coastal marshes within a mile of the Gulf of Mexico.

Behavior Specific behavior of this frog is not known, but it is believed to be similar to other cricket frogs.

Reproduction Unknown.

Canyon Treefrog

Hyla arenicolor

Description 1¼ to 2¼ inches total length. This generally brownish gray frog has indistinct dorsal markings varying from dark brown to ash gray. The rough skin may be tinged with pink. The hidden surfaces of the thigh are marked with bright yellow-orange. Below the eye, it has a light spot with dark edges. On the male, the throat is dark. Ventral surfaces of both sexes are creamy, grading to yellow near the hind legs. This treefrog has a distinct toadlike appearance, with its warty skin and rounded shape. Its coloration provides effective camouflage in its rocky environment. It has large toe pads, and the webbing on the hind foot is well developed.

Voice The vocal sac has 2 lobes, and the call is a series of abrupt nasal, hollow-sounding notes all of the same pitch. The effect of the 1- to 3-second calls is that of an explosive whirring.

Range Found in the Chisos and Davis mountains of the Trans-Pecos region.

Habitat Although its range includes arid and semiarid regions, this treefrog is never far from water. It prefers locations near permanent watercourses with rocky pools. It may be found in canyons or in wooded areas.

Behavior This treefrog spends most of its time on the ground among or on the rocks near water, but it may climb low trees or shrubs near the water. It is primarily nocturnal and hides during daylight in rock crevices. It can also be seen in niches on the sides of large rocks, within jumping distance from water. When threatened, it may flatten against the rock and be quite invisible because of its coloration. If it retreats to water, it will soon return to nearby rocks.

Reproduction Breeding takes place from March through July when rains are adequate. It usually deposits eggs singly, enclosed in a jelly envelope, in quiet water of rock-lined streams. They attach to vegetation or debris or rocks on the bottom, or they may float on the surface.

Cope's Gray Treefrog

Hyla chrysoscelis

Note This species and the gray treefrog, *Hyla versicolor,* are identical in their physical descriptions, as well as range, habitat, and behavior patterns. They are distinguished from each other only by differences in their calls and by their chromosome counts. In the field, observers can make the distinction only by carefully monitoring the calls. *H. chrysoscelis* has the faster trill, but without comparison the calls may be difficult to tell apart. The chromosome count of *H. versicolor* is twice that of *H. chrysoscelis.*

Description 1¼ to 2⅜ inches total length. This treefrog is well camouflaged with its coloration of green or brown to gray. It has several large dark blotches on its back that may be interpreted as an irregular cross shape. It usually has a dark-edged light spot under the eye. The legs usually have dark bars, and the hidden surfaces of the hind legs are bright yellow-orange. Its skin is rough with small warts. It has large pads on the tips of its long toes.

Voice The call is a fast, high-pitched musical trill. It can be heard in the spring and early summer during breeding.

Range Found throughout the eastern half of the state, not including the Rio Grande Valley.

Habitat It is at home in wooded areas along creeks and rivers, where trees and shrubs overhang or grow in the water.

Behavior This primarily nocturnal treefrog lives most of its life in the trees or shrubs near or in shallow water. It descends only to chorus and to breed.

Reproduction Breeding takes place from mid-March through July or even later in warmer areas. Tadpoles transform at about ⅝ inch.

Green Treefrog
Hyla cinerea

Description   1¼ to 2½ inches total length. This angular treefrog is usually bright green, but color can vary depending on season, from yellow during breeding to dark gray when it is inactive in cold weather. It normally has a distinct white or pale yellow stripe on its side from the jaw to the groin. The length of the stripe varies, and it is sometimes absent. Many individuals have small gold flecks on their backs. Its body is slim, smooth, and flat. The head is pointed and flat, with prominent eyes. The lips are white, and sometimes the white of the lips is connected to the side stripe. Legs are long, and toe pads are large.

Voice   The vocal sac is round, and the call is a bell-like, ringing sound repeated up to 75 times per minute. The call is loud, and often hundreds of males will call together, all clinging to shrubs and leaf stems overhanging the water. It is locally called a rain frog because it seems to call mostly during humid weather.

Range   Found throughout the eastern third of the state, from the Oklahoma and Arkansas borders south to the Gulf of Mexico, and in an isolated locale in the extreme tip of the Lower Rio Grande Valley.

Habitat   It is at home wherever there is water with sandy banks and dense vegetation. It can be seen in swamps, along streams and rivers, or around the edges of lakes. It requires vegetation in and near the water. It is often seen around human habitations where conditions are appropriate.

Behavior   It calls most often just before dark, congregating in large choruses. It lives on leaves and stems in or near water, seeking shelter under the leaves when threatened. It eats a variety of insects and may be drawn to lighted windows where insects are likely to be present. It will usually walk rather than jump, but it will take awkward leaps into space to avoid capture.

Reproduction   Breeding takes place from March to October, and it drops its eggs in small jelly packets that attach to floating vegetation. Tadpoles transform after 55 to 63 days.

Squirrel Treefrog

Hyla squirella

Description   ⅞ to 1⅝ inches total length of head and body. This small frog has smooth skin and prominent eyes. General coloration varies widely, and an individual may change colors. Dorsal surfaces may be bright green, olive, or any of several shades of brown. The back and legs may be spotted, but spots may be absent. It often has a broken dark band running across the head between the eyes. It usually has a whitish stripe along the upper jaw. A separate, less distinct white line may extend down the side of the body. And it may have small yellow flecks on the back. Toe pads are large.

Voice   This frog has 2 calls, one of which has provided its name. It calls just before or during rains, in a scolding, raspy chatter like that of a squirrel. Its breeding call is different: a nasal, quacking trill repeated at a rate of 1 or 2 per second. It usually calls while clinging to a vertical stem hanging low over water.

Range   Found within a wide band in the southeastern part of the state, from the Louisiana border along the coast to Corpus Christi Bay.

Habitat   This frog is at home in a variety of habitats, anywhere with sufficient moisture, insect prey, and suitable hiding places. It is most often seen in gardens or in wooded areas with tangled underbrush.

Behavior   Primarily nocturnal, this active little frog is an aggressive predator, and it may fall from trees while pursuing insect prey. In dry weather, it seeks shelter during the day in hollow tree limbs, under loose bark, or in garden shrubs. It may often be seen hiding under the eaves of houses, sometimes in groups. During rainy weather, it may be abroad in daylight, especially after a heavy downpour. It will sound its "rain call" during the day and is commonly referred to as the rain frog.

Reproduction   Breeding takes place from March to October, and it lays eggs singly on the bottom of shallow pools. Tadpoles transform after 40 to 50 days.

Gray Treefrog
Hyla versicolor

Note This species and Cope's gray treefrog, *Hyla chrysoscelis,* are identical in their physical descriptions, as well as range, habitat, and behavior patterns. They are distinguished from each other only by differences in their calls and by their chromosome counts. In the field, observers can make the distinction only by carefully monitoring the calls. *H. chrysoscelis* has the faster trill, but without comparison the calls may be difficult to tell apart. The chromosome count of *H. versicolor* is twice that of *H. chrysoscelis.*

Description 1¼ to 2⅜ inches total length. This treefrog is well camouflaged with its coloration of green or brown to gray. It has several large dark blotches on its back that may be interpreted as an irregular cross shape. It usually has a dark-edged light spot under the eye. The legs usually have dark bars, and the hidden surfaces of the hind legs are bright yellow-orange. Its skin is rough with small warts. It has large pads on the tips of its long toes.

Voice The call is a high-pitched musical trill, slower than that of *H. chrysoscelis.* It can be heard in the spring and early summer during breeding.

Range Found throughout the eastern half of the state, not including the Rio Grande Valley.

Habitat It is at home in wooded areas along creeks and rivers, where trees and shrubs overhang or grow in the water.

Behavior This primarily nocturnal treefrog lives most of its life in the trees or shrubs near or in shallow water. It descends only to chorus and to breed.

Reproduction Breeding takes place from mid-March through July or even later in warmer areas. Tadpoles transform at about ⅝ inch.

Spotted Chorus Frog

Pseudacris clarkii

Description ¾ to 1¼ inches total length of head and body. This small frog is slender and has a long snout. Its skin is evenly textured with many small rounded warts. General coloration is pale gray-brown or ash, and pattern varies from a scattering of black-rimmed bright green spots to stripes formed when the spots line up and fuse longitudinally. A black-rimmed green stripe runs from the snout through the eye and onto the shoulder, sometimes down the side. The frog usually has a green triangular spot between the eyes with the apex pointing backward. The ventral surfaces are white and plain, and toe pads are round and small.

Voice The call is a rapidly repeated series of rasping trills, with intervals between calls the same length as the call. When several males are heard at a distance, the call sounds like sawing.

Range Found throughout a wide swath down the middle of the state, from the central Panhandle south to the eastern Rio Grande Valley.

Habitat It is at home on prairies, but usually stays in marshy areas near watercourses.

Behavior Primarily nocturnal, it may also be active at twilight, but only during rainy weather. It is inactive in dry weather.

Reproduction Breeding takes place year-round in the southern part of the state, but only after rains. Elsewhere it breeds in late spring, with a peak during April and May, during spring rains.

Northern Spring Peeper

Pseudacris crucifer crucifer

Description   ¾ to 1⅜ inches total length of head and body. This small frog is relatively long and slender with smooth skin. It has large toe pads on unwebbed toes. General coloration varies widely. It may be any of several shades of brown from light tan to rosy, or it may be gray or olive. Females are lighter in general color than males. The ventral surfaces are pale and unmarked. Most individuals have dark markings on the back that form a distinctive X shape.

Voice   The vocal sac on males is large, and the call is a series of high-pitched whistles of a single note, sometimes with a short trill, that are repeated at 1-second intervals. A large chorus may be heard at a great distance, and the combined effect has been compared to the sound of sleigh bells.

Range   Found throughout the extreme eastern part of the state, from the Oklahoma and Arkansas borders south to the Gulf of Mexico.

Habitat   It is at home in moist wooded areas with streams or ponds, in open marshy areas, or in swamps near the source of water.

Behavior   Primarily nocturnal, it may be abroad in daylight during rainy weather. It is seldom seen except during the breeding season, when groups of individuals form choruses in trees and upright grasses in or near water. During very cold weather it hibernates under fallen logs or other vegetative debris. Its call is always one of the first signs of spring.

Reproduction   Breeding takes place early, depending on the weather, sometimes beginning in late November and continuing through February or early March. It lays eggs singly among vegetation underwater. Tadpoles transform after 90 to 100 days.

Strecker's Chorus Frog

Pseudacris streckeri streckeri

Description 1 to 1⅝ inches. This small, plump frog has a toadlike shape, and its coloration is highly variable, from pale gray to rich brown. Most individuals have a dark line from the snout, through the eye, and onto the shoulder, and most have a dark spot below the eye. Dorsal pattern varies from quite plain to many large spots of brown or green in sharp contrast to the ground color. Individuals with relatively unmarked dorsal surfaces will usually have some spotting along the sides. The groin is often yellowish. Its head is short and wide, and its forelegs are short and stout. Its toes are slightly webbed and have small round disks at the tips.

Voice Calls can be heard from December or January until May, usually during and after rains. The call is a single, bell-like note rapidly repeated, and in a large chorus it can sound like the turning of a wheel in need of grease.

Range Found from the Oklahoma border south through most of the central and eastern part of the state to the Gulf of Mexico.

Habitat This frog is at home in a variety of habitats but prefers moist areas, including woods and open fields, as well as rocky ravines, all with sources of moisture nearby. It may also be seen in swamps and in or near streams.

Behavior This robust frog is nocturnal, and it burrows with its sturdy front feet when seeking shelter from heat or predation.

Reproduction Breeding takes place from midwinter through spring, and it deposits up to 700 eggs in water, where they attach to vegetation. The tadpoles transform in about 60 days.

Upland Chorus Frog

Pseudacris triseriata feriarum

Description   ¾ to 1½ inches. This small, slender frog has a long, pointed head and fine, granular skin. General coloration varies from pale gray-brown to olive, and dorsal pattern is variable, from 3 dark stripes to pale stripes to stripes broken into spots. Dorsal pattern may be lacking altogether. Two constant characteristics are the white line along the upper lip and the dark stripe that runs from the snout, through the eye, and onto the side to the groin. Many individuals have a dark triangle on top of the head, with the apex pointing backward. The toes are slender and have little webbing and small disks. One toe on each foot is much longer than the others.

Voice   Males call from floating vegetation, often out in the open, and the call is a raspy rising trill that lasts about 2 seconds.

Range   Found throughout the eastern third of the state, from the Oklahoma and Arkansas borders south to the Gulf of Mexico and south along the coast to about Corpus Christi.

Habitat   This frog is at home in a variety of habitats, from dry grassy areas to river-bottom swamps. It is found in woodlands and in cultivated fields, as well as near ponds and marshes. In spite of its name, it may be found in lowland regions. Throughout its range, it is adapted to areas of human habitation.

Behavior   It is nocturnal and shy, disappearing beneath the surface of water or other convenient shelter when approached.

Reproduction   Breeding takes place from midwinter through spring, usually in shallow pools either out in the open or in woods.

Mexican Treefrog
Smilisca baudinii

Description 2 to 3⅝ inches total length of head and body. This large treefrog has smooth skin and large toe pads. General coloration varies widely, from light green, gray, or yellow to dark brown or gray. An individual may change its color and pattern. It has a dark line running from the snout through the eye onto the shoulder area, usually ending in a blotch. It may have other brown blotches on the back and sides. Lighter colored individuals usually do not have brown blotches on the back. It usually has a light spot beneath the eye. At rest, the body forms a dramatic V shape.

Voice The inflated vocal sac of males creates 2 bulges extending down and out from the throat. The call is a series of short, abrupt notes of a medium pitch. A chuckle may be interspersed among the notes. The notes are repeated 5 to 12 times in 2 or 3 seconds, with intervals between calls of about 2 or 3 seconds.

Range Found in the extreme southern tip of the state in the Lower Rio Grande Valley. There is one historical record of this species in Bexar County, but the frog may no longer be there.

Habitat It is at home in humid places in arid and semiarid regions, such as along streams, resacas, and roadside ditches. It prefers areas with trees or shrubs. In areas with banana trees, it will hide in the outer sheaths, and it has been observed living in the tops of tall palms.

Behavior It is nocturnal and seeks shelter from heat and sun under loose tree bark, in holes in trees, or in damp soil.

Reproduction Breeding takes place year-round, whenever sufficient rain falls.

Eastern Barking Frog

Hylactophryne augusti latrans

Description   2½ to 3¾ inches maximum length. This frog has a distinctly toadlike shape, with a large head and large forelegs. Its skin is smooth, and general coloration varies widely from tan to green to gray and may even be pinkish or purplish. It has dark blotches with light borders scattered over the dorsal surfaces. Its toes are slender and unwebbed, with small toe pads and large tubercles under each joint. Distinctive characteristics include folds on each side of the back, a fold across the back of the head, and a disk-shaped fold on the belly.

Voice   The call is a single explosive note repeated at regular intervals of 2 to 3 seconds, and at a distance it sounds like the barking of a dog.

Range   Found in a narrow crescent from Central Texas to the Rio Grande to the corner of New Mexico.

Habitat   This frog frequents damp areas in limestone caves, crevices and ledges. It is rarely seen in the open.

Behavior   This nocturnal frog is secretive in its habitat. It is terrestrial and a dexterous rock climber. It walks with its entire body held high off the ground, and when captured or threatened it will inflate its body to several times its normal size.

Reproduction   Breeding takes place from February to May during rainy periods. It lays eggs under rocks or logs in moist earth, and tadpoles transform inside the eggs, emerging as frogs.

White-lipped Frog
Leptodactylus fragilis

Description   1⅜ to 2 inches. This angular frog has a pointed head with prominent eyes. General coloration varies from gray to brown with variable dark dorsal spots. It has a white or cream-colored line along its upper lip. The toes are long and have no toe pads. Identifying characteristics include folds low on each side of the back and a distinct disk on its belly.

Voice   The call is formed of 2 notes, with the second note rising in pitch. It has a generally throaty tone. Males call from underneath clumps of grass or dirt clods or from small depressions.

Range   Found only in the extreme southern edge of the Lower Rio Grande Valley.

Habitat   This frog is at home in a variety of habitats wherever sufficient moisture exists. It may be seen in cultivated fields, especially those that are irrigated, in the surrounding irrigation ditches, in low grasslands, and in runoff areas.

Behavior   This nocturnal frog burrows in damp soil, where it hides during the day. It forages in the open at night. The male may excavate small depressions to catch rain in which the female will deposit eggs.

Reproduction   Breeding takes place in spring when heavy rains fill small pools, forming the right environment for nests. The frog creates nests by whipping body secretions into a foam, then lays eggs in the foam. If excavations dry up, the eggs survive in the liquid center of the foamy nest until the next rain.

Rio Grande Chirping Frog

Syrrhophus cystignathoides campi

Description ⅝ to 1 inch maximum length. This tiny frog has an elongated, flattened body, pointed snout, well-developed forelegs, and long, slender toes with prominent tubercles and truncated toe pads that are more noticeable on the front feet than on the rear. General coloration is brown, gray, or yellowish green, and there are dark spots scattered on the fine granular skin of the back. The legs are crossbarred, and there is a dark smudged line from the nostril through the eye. The skin on the ventral surfaces is translucent, and the dark line of a blood vessel is visible through the skin down the middle of the belly.

Voice Calls are not loud, but they can be heard most of the year whenever it rains. The sound is an abrupt cricketlike chirp consisting of 1 or 2 notes repeated at irregular intervals.

Range Found in the extreme southern tip of the Lower Rio Grande Valley.

Habitat This delicate frog is at home in the natural environment of moist palm groves, thickets of underbrush, or resacas. It is also well adapted to areas of human habitation, including well-watered lawns, flower beds and gardens, rain gutters, irrigation ditches, and rubbish piles.

Behavior A nocturnal frog, it can easily be discovered in daylight in its hiding places under loose boards, rocks, or moist vegetative debris. But though easily found, it is not easily captured, because it is quick and will leap, hop, or run for shelter. It may burrow in moist earth.

Reproduction Breeding takes place in April and May. The female lays fewer than 12 large eggs, and tadpoles probably transform inside the egg.

Spotted Chirping Frog

Syrrhophus guttilatus

Description ¾ to 1¼ inches maximum length. This small frog has a large, broad head with nostrils close to the tip of the short snout. Its smooth skin is yellowish brown with an overall dark brown wormlike pattern. The legs have dark crossbars, and there is a dark bar between the eyes. The toes have truncated pads that are more prominent on the front than on the rear.

Voice The call is an abrupt, short whistle of a single note.

Range This frog is found in 2 small locales in the Big Bend region.

Habitat It is at home in canyons, ravines, and caves near sources of water, especially at the mouth of springs.

Behavior This nocturnal frog can be distinguished by its tendency to walk rather than hop or leap. It jumps only to evade predators but is more likely to run. It may burrow in moist earth or hide under rocks and leaf litter during the day. At night it feeds on insects, spiders, and small crustaceans.

Reproduction Breeding takes place from late winter through spring, and it lays fewer than 15 eggs.

Cliff Chirping Frog

Syrrhophus marnockii

Description   ¾ to 1½ inches maximum length. This small frog has a flattened body and a long flattened head with a broad space between the prominent eyes. Its smooth skin is greenish and has scattered brown spots interspersed with light flecks. The delicate legs are crossbarred, and the long, slender toes have prominent tubercles and truncated toe pads.

Voice   Calls can be heard throughout most of the year, and they consist of 1 or 2 brief notes like the chirp of a cricket, sometimes followed by a trill of 2 or 3 notes. In the presence of females, males call in sharper, clearer tones.

Range   Found in Central Texas and in a wide band westward to the Rio Grande.

Habitat   It is adapted to life in caves and crevices of the limestone hills within its range.

Behavior   A nocturnal frog, it may leap, hop, or run to seek shelter. It is quick and evades capture easily by slipping into cracks in the limestone.

Reproduction   Breeding may take place from February to December, with the peak season in April and May. Females may lay eggs 3 times a year, and tadpoles probably transform within the egg.

Eastern Narrowmouth Toad

Gastrophryne carolinensis

Description ⅞ to 1½ inches maximum length. This tiny, plump toad is smooth-skinned, with a small head, a pointed snout, an egg-shaped body, and stout limbs. It has a fold of skin across the back of the head just behind the eyes. General coloration varies from gray to brown to reddish, and an individual may change color depending on environment. The center of the back is usually dark, and there may be lighter dorsolateral stripes and mottling with dark spots. The ventral surfaces are strongly mottled. The throat of the male is dark. There is a single enlarged tubercle, or spade, on each hind foot, and the toes are not webbed.

Voice Males call while floating in water with their forefeet resting on some support. The call is a lively, though not loud, bleating, and it lasts ½ to 4 seconds.

Range Found in most of the eastern half of the state.

Habitat This toad requires ample moisture and cover and thus is always near water, for instance at the edges of ponds and ditches where fallen logs or other debris provide adequate hiding places.

Behavior It is a skillful burrower, and though it usually hides during the day under logs, debris, or rocks, it sometimes emerges in heavy rain. It eats ants and a variety of insects.

Reproduction Breeding takes place from May through September and is initiated by rains. The female deposits eggs as a film on the surface of the water.

Great Plains Narrowmouth Toad

Gastrophryne olivacea

Description   ⅞ to 1⅝ inches maximum length. This tiny, plump toad has an egg-shaped, neckless body and a pointed snout on its small head. Its skin is smooth, and it has a fold of skin across the back of the head just behind its small eyes. Its legs are slender and toes unwebbed, and each hind foot has a well-developed tubercle, or spade. Coloration varies from light tan to gray to olive and may change depending on the environment of the individual. The back may have a scattering of small black spots. The ventral surfaces are light and unmarked, except that on males the throat is dark.

Voice   The call is a high-pitched, though not loud, bleating with a buzzing resonance. Duration of a call is 1 to 4 seconds.

Range   Found throughout most of the state, except for the eastern border, the western tip, and the Panhandle.

Habitat   It prefers moist areas in grasslands or woods with rodent burrows, which it may use for shelter.

Behavior   This nocturnal toad feeds mainly on ants and hides in moist places under rocks or debris. It may burrow in with a tarantula, rodent, or reptile.

Reproduction   Breeding takes place from March to September when rains create pools and fill ditches. The female lays eggs in a film on the surface of the water.

Sheep Frog
Hypopachus variolosus

Description 1 to 1¾ inches maximum length. This small frog has a round shape, with no neck and a pointed snout. Its skin is smooth, and it has a fold of skin across its head just behind the small eyes. The toes are slightly webbed, and each hind foot has 2 prominent enlarged tubercles, or spades. General coloration is olive to brown, sometimes with dark spots or streaks, and the frog is distinguished by a thin yellow line from the snout down the length of the back. The ventral surfaces are gray and may have some dark mottling, and there is a thin white line down the length of the belly with a branch across each side of the chest to the forelegs. The throat of the male is dark.

Voice The call is a clear, resonant bleating lasting about 2 seconds at intervals of not less than 15 seconds.

Range Found in far South Texas and in the Lower Rio Grande Valley.

Habitat This frog is at home in arid areas, but it prefers moist subterranean burrows, such as those of the pack rat or those created by fallen and partially buried tree trunks or limbs. It frequents the edges of ponds or irrigation ditches, hiding under vegetative debris.

Behavior This frog is difficult to observe because it remains hidden under debris or in burrows for most of the year, coming out only at night during or after rains. It feeds on ants and termites.

Reproduction Breeding takes place from March to September when rain or irrigation creates pools and fills ditches. Eggs float on the surface of the water, and they hatch within 24 hours. Tadpoles transform in about 4 weeks.

Plains Spadefoot

Scaphiopus bombifrons

Description   1½ to 2½ inches maximum length at maturity. This stout spadefoot toad is distinguished by the prominent bony boss between its eyes, which are large and have vertical pupils. General coloration on the relatively smooth skin varies from gray to brown and may even be greenish. The dorsal surfaces may be reticulated with dark brown or gray, and the small tubercles or warts may be yellowish or reddish and encircled by dark pigment. The ventral surfaces are white. Some individuals may have 4 vague white stripes on the back. Each hind foot has a short, dark, rounded, wedge-shaped spade on the inside surface, which is used for digging. The toes are webbed.

Voice   The usual call is a short, resonant squawk or raspy bleat lasting ½ to ¾ second and given at intervals of ½ to 1 second. Another call is a low-pitched, raspy trill lasting 1 second.

Range   Found in the Panhandle and throughout the far western part of the state and in a separate population in the southern tip.

Habitat   It is well adapted to life in arid regions, preferring sandy soil for easy burrowing. It is at home on plains, shortgrass prairies, and cultivated farmland. It may be seen near temporary or permanent pools.

Behavior   This nocturnal toad is a prodigious burrower, pushing the loose soil aside with its spades and rocking slowly backward into the earth. It can bury itself quickly as the sand falls in around it. The burrows are dug down to depths of several feet, and sometimes a sticky substance will be seen at the entrance. The toad may stay underground for long periods, coming to the surface only on rainy nights.

Reproduction   Breeding takes place from May to August when rains create temporary pools. Eggs are deposited in a mass and attach to underwater vegetation. They hatch within 48 hours, and the tadpoles must transform quickly, before their temporary pools dry up. Also, they are omnivorous and may eat each other.

Couch's Spadefoot
Scaphiopus couchii

Description   2¼ to 3½ inches maximum length at maturity. This stout toad has large eyes with vertical pupils and no boss between the eyes. General coloration varies from bright greenish yellow to brownish yellow. The dorsal surfaces are covered with an irregular mottling of dark green or brown or black. The skin is covered with many small warts, some light-colored and some quite dark. Ventral surfaces are white. Each hind foot has a dark, elongated, sickle-shaped spade used for digging in sandy soil.

Voice   The call is a plaintive bleat, like a distressed lamb, lasting up to a full second and declining in pitch. A large chorus can be heard at great distances.

Range   Found throughout most of the state except for the eastern third.

Habitat   An inhabitant of shortgrass prairies and mesquite savannahs, this toad is adapted to arid or semiarid regions.

Behavior   This nocturnal toad burrows deep into sandy or gravelly soil and may stay underground for long periods. It also seeks shelter under fallen logs or other debris. Males call from the rims of temporary pools.

Reproduction   Breeding takes place in temporary pools from April to September after heavy rainfall. The female lays eggs in cylindrical masses that attach to plant stems underwater. Hatching occurs within 36 hours, and tadpoles transform in 2 to 6 weeks before pools evaporate.

Hurter's Spadefoot

Scaphiopus holbrookii hurterii

Description   1¾ to 3¼ inches maximum length at maturity. This toad has a stout body, a short, wide head with a blunt snout, and a prominent boss between and a little behind its large eyes. General coloration is grayish green to brown to nearly black, usually with 2 irregular light lines down the length of the back. Ventral surfaces are white or pale gray. The relatively smooth skin has a scattering of small tubercles or warts. On each hind foot is a dark, elongated, sickle-shaped spade used for digging in sandy soil.

Voice   The call is an abrupt low-pitched bleat of short duration, with intervals of about 2 seconds between calls. A large chorus can be heard at great distances.

Range   Found throughout the eastern half of the state, including the eastern part of South Texas.

Habitat   This toad can be found in arid and semiarid regions, but it more typically prefers sandy, gravelly soil in wooded areas or cultivated farmland.

Behavior   A nocturnal toad, it remains most of the time in shallow burrows that it digs with the spades on its hind feet, pushing soil aside and rocking slowly backward into the earth.

Reproduction   Breeding takes place from March to September after rains create temporary pools. The female lays eggs in bands that attach to underwater vegetation. They hatch within 48 hours, and tadpoles transform in 2 to 8 weeks, before pools dry up.

Southern Spadefoot
Scaphiopus multiplicatus

Description 1½ to 2½ inches maximum length. This stout-bodied toad has a broad head with a short snout and no boss between the eyes. Its large eyes have vertical pupils. General coloration is gray or brown, sometimes deep green or even black. The lighter colors have a scattering of irregular dark spots, and the relatively smooth skin has many small tubercles or warts tipped in orange or yellow. Some individuals may have 4 vague longitudinal light-colored stripes. The ventral surfaces are white. Each of the hind feet has a short, dark, wedge-shaped spade used for digging in sandy or gravelly soil.

Voice The call is a lively trill, sometimes compared to the purr of a cat or to the sound of a fingernail dragged along the teeth of a comb. Each trill lasts ¾ to 1½ seconds.

Range Found in the Panhandle and throughout West Texas.

Habitat Adapted to a variety of conditions, this toad is at home on shortgrass prairies, floodplains, alkali flats, and areas with open vegetation. It prefers loose, sandy soil for easy digging. It tolerates arid and semiarid conditions but usually is not found in desert areas.

Behavior This nocturnal toad burrows deep into sandy, gravelly soil. It uses its spades to push dirt aside in a rocking motion, backing into the hole. The soil usually falls in as the toad digs deeper.

Reproduction Breeding takes place in temporary pools and quiet streams from January to August during periods of rainfall. Eggs are laid in cylindrical masses that attach to underwater vegetation. They hatch within 48 hours, and tadpoles transform in 4 to 6 weeks before pools evaporate. The tadpoles eat mosquito larvae and may eat each other.

Southern Crawfish Frog

Rana areolata areolata

Description   2¼ to 4½ inches maximum length at maturity. This stocky frog has a large head and relatively rough skin covered with round, dark spots with light borders. General coloration varies from brown to black, depending on temperature and activity, and the dark spots sometimes join to create irregular bands across the back. The ventral surfaces are white and usually unspotted. The concealed surfaces of the groin and hind legs are yellowish. Prominent dorsolateral folds may also be yellowish. Its legs are relatively short, and the toes on the rear feet are extensively webbed, with webbing extending about half the length of the longest toe.

Voice   The call is a deep, guttural trill with great resonance and carrying power, especially in chorus.

Range   Found in the center of East Texas and south to about halfway down the coastline. A separate population occupies a narrow band along the Red River.

Habitat   This frog is at home in pine forests and meadows with abundant moisture. It usually inhabits abandoned crawfish holes with the castle tops missing, but it also uses mammal burrows and storm sewers.

Behavior   This nocturnal frog seldom ventures far beyond the entrance to its daytime hiding place, except during breeding, when it may travel great distances. It eats almost anything, including insects and other frogs, but prefers crawfish.

Reproduction   Breeding may take place year-round, with the peak of the season from February to June. Egg masses are laid in shallow water, and sometimes they attach to underwater vegetation.

Rio Grande Leopard Frog

Rana berlandieri

Description 2¼ to 4½ inches maximum length. This angular, alert frog is light green to tan, with large dark spots between light-colored dorsolateral ridges. The ridges are prominent, and a significant characteristic is that they are broken and inset slightly at the hip. There may be a light stripe along the upper jaw, but it is often poorly defined. This slim-waisted frog has smooth skin and long, sturdy legs.

Voice The call is a low-pitched, short, rapid guttural trill, with a rate of about 13 per second. The paired vocal sacs, when deflated, fold into a pouch on each side that appears as a dark slit.

Range Found throughout Central, far West, and South Texas.

Habitat Though this frog is adapted to fairly arid conditions, it prefers areas with moisture, such as along streams or rivers and near cattle tanks, ponds, or ditches.

Behavior Primarily nocturnal, this frog burrows under rocks to find shelter from the sun and heat. When approached, it may take refuge in scrub brush or cactus, if water is not conveniently nearby. It will eat a variety of insects, as well as most anything else smaller than itself.

Reproduction Breeding takes place anytime year-round after rains. Egg masses are deposited in water and attach to submerged vegetation.

Plains Leopard Frog

Rana blairi

Description 2 to 4⅜ inches maximum length. This stocky frog is green to brown, with large dark spots between prominent yellowish dorsolateral ridges, which are broken at the hip and inset slightly. It has a distinct light line along the upper jaw, and it usually has a light spot on the eardrum. The groin and underside of the thigh are yellow. The eyes are large, and the snout is fairly pointed. The hind legs are long, and the long toes are extensively webbed.

Voice The call is made up of 2 or 3 distinctly spaced guttural notes per second. The paired vocal sacs are concealed in small, roughened longitudinal slits on each side, under the jaw.

Range Found in the Panhandle and the north-central part of the state.

Habitat Adapted to the dry conditions of prairies and open plains, it seeks out grassy areas with some moisture, such as along streams, the edges of ponds, and marshes.

Behavior Primarily nocturnal, this frog may occasionally forage on cloudy days for its diet of insects and most anything smaller than itself.

Reproduction Breeding takes place anytime year-round with sufficient warm rain.

Bullfrog
Rana catesbeiana

Description 3½ to 8 inches record maximum length at maturity. This is the largest of the frogs. General coloration varies from olive to green to brown, and there may be dark gray or brown spotting on the back. The long, powerful hind legs may be banded or blotched. The ventral surfaces are pale with a yellow tinge, and some gray mottling may be present. The skin is somewhat roughened with fine tubercles. The body is broad, and the tympanum is prominent, with a ridge running from behind the eye, around the tympanum, and down to just behind the jaw. The ridges do not continue onto the trunk. The hind feet are fully webbed, except for the fourth toe, which extends beyond the webbing.

Voice The bullfrog has a single, internal vocal sac, which inflates to enormous size during calls. When deflated, it forms a flat pouch under the chin. The distinctive call is a deep-pitched series of 3 notes, which sound to many like "jug-o'-rum." The call, commonly heard in the evenings of early summer, carries more than a quarter of a mile.

Range Found throughout most of the state, except for the mountain ranges in the west.

Habitat The bullfrog prefers large bodies of water, but it must have sufficient shallows with vegetation for cover and for breeding. It may be seen around lakes, ponds, or cattle tanks or in slow-moving streams.

Behavior This aquatic frog is active in the evening and at night, and it usually stays in the vegetation at water's edge. Its activity is not dependent on rainfall, since it never strays from bodies of water. It is solitary and, during breeding, territorial. It can leap distances of many times its body length. It eats insects, crawfish, minnows, and other frogs, as well as small birds and snakes.

Reproduction Breeding takes place from February to October. The female lays egg masses on the surface of the water in a film, then they drift down into the water and attach to vegetation. As many as 20,000 eggs may be laid at once, and tadpoles transform slowly, taking as long as 2 years.

Bronze Frog

Rana clamitans clamitans

Description   2⅛ to 3⅜ inches maximum length at maturity. This frog has relatively smooth skin, and coloration varies from pale brown to deep bronze. Ventral surfaces are whitish and usually have thin, irregular dark lines or spots. Males may have yellowish throats, and both sexes may have green on the upper lip. The eyes are quite large, and the tympanum is prominent. Prominent dorsolateral ridges run from just behind the eye, over the tympanum, and onto the trunk, but not to the groin. The ridges may curve down behind the tympanum and may be broken posteriorly. The hind legs are long, as are the toes, with the fourth toe extending well beyond the webbing.

Voice   The paired vocal sacs are internal, and both the throat and the sacs expand during calls. The call is a single abrupt twang of medium pitch that sounds like the plucking of a string on a musical instrument. The note may be repeated 3 or 4 times in rapid succession.

Range   Found throughout East Texas, from the Oklahoma and Arkansas borders to the Gulf of Mexico, and into east-central Texas.

Habitat   This frog must have a moist environment and stays near shallow water, such as swamps, slow-moving streams, and the margins of lakes or ponds. It is usually seen in the debris of fallen limbs and tree trunks near the water.

Behavior   This primarily nocturnal frog is usually under shelter but is not especially alarmed when approached. It tends to be solitary.

Reproduction   Breeding takes place from March to August, and the female lays eggs in small masses that attach to submerged vegetation.

Pig Frog
Rana grylio

Description 3¼ to 6⅜ inches maximum length at maturity. This large frog is similar to the bullfrog. It has hefty legs and body, and the eyes and tympanum are prominent. General coloration varies from yellow-green to gray-green to brown, often with many dark spots. Ventral surfaces are white with a yellow tinge, and there may be a dark mottling posteriorly and on the legs. The hind legs may be banded. The head is narrow and pointed. A prominent ridge starting just behind the eye curves over and down behind the tympanum and ends just behind the jaw. There are no dorsolateral ridges on the body. The hind legs and toes are long, and the toes are fully webbed, even to the tip of the fourth toe, distinguishing it from the bullfrog.

Voice The internal vocal sac, when inflated, creates a 3-part appearance, with the vocal sac expanding to the sides as the throat also enlarges. Calls can be heard throughout most of the year, and males usually call while floating in shallow water. The call is an abrupt low-pitched grunt, and a large chorus produces a loud, steady roar.

Range Found in the extreme southeastern corner of the state.

Habitat The pig frog must have an aquatic environment, such as marshes and cypress bogs and the margins of lakes or ponds. It requires dense vegetation in the water, both floating and submerged.

Behavior This frog is primarily nocturnal, but it may be active on very cloudy days. It is wary and difficult to approach, remaining hidden in floating vegetation, such as water lilies and cattails. It feeds primarily on crawfish, but it may also eat minnows, smaller frogs, or snakes. Large males are territorial and call to defend territory, as well as during breeding.

Reproduction Breeding takes place from March through September. The tadpoles are quite large, as are those of the bullfrog, and take up to 2 years to transform.

Pickerel Frog

Rana palustris

Description 1¾ to 3⁷⁄₁₆ inches maximum length at maturity. This slender, long-legged frog is tan or light brown and elaborately marked with large, almost square dark spots on its back. The spots are usually arranged in 4 distinct rows, with 2 down the middle of the back, between pale dorsolateral ridges, and 1 on each side. The spots may be reddish brown, usually darker at the edges, and rimmed in white. The hind legs are distinctly banded. There is usually a dark streak from the nostril to the eye and a light line along the upper jaw. The ventral surfaces are yellow, with tinges of orange in the folds of the thighs, and have a mottling of dark lines or spots. The skin is smooth, and poisonous skin-gland secretions make this frog unappealing to many of its predators.

Voice This frog has 2 vocal sacs. Its call is a low-pitched croak lasting 1 or 2 seconds, and it may call while completely submerged, creating a sound like a gurgling snore.

Range Found throughout East Texas.

Habitat The moist habitats of this frog include the coastal plains and floodplains along rivers, as well as swamps or other damp locations with plenty of vegetation in the water. It may also be seen in meadows and woods away from water.

Behavior Primarily nocturnal, this frog hibernates from about October until March or April. When captured, it will secrete a toxic substance that is highly irritating if exposed to a cut or rubbed in the eyes. The secretion may cause some irritation on any exposed skin surfaces.

Reproduction Breeding takes place as soon as frogs emerge from hibernation in March or April and continues through May. Eggs are laid in water, and the egg masses attach to submerged vegetation.

Southern Leopard Frog

Rana sphenocephala

Description   2 to 5 inches record maximum length at maturity. This slender frog has a narrow, pointed head and long hind legs and toes. General coloration varies from tan to several shades of brown to green, and an individual may have a combination of these colors. The back is usually covered with dark brown spots between distinct light-colored dorsolateral ridges, and the sides may have some spotting. Large brown spots on the legs may create the effect of bands. It has a light line along the upper jaw and usually a light spot in the center of the tympanum.

Voice   The paired vocal sacs, when deflated, form pouches under the jaw on either side. During calls, the sacs inflate to spheres. The call is a rapid series of abrupt, deep croaks, creating a guttural trill. The trill rate may be as much as 13 per second. Males will call from land or while floating in shallow water.

Range   Found throughout East Texas and into the south-central region.

Habitat   This frog prefers the environs of shallow water, but it may be seen some distance from water if there is sufficient vegetation to provide protection. A distinguishing characteristic is its ability to live in brackish marshes along the coast.

Behavior   This frog skillfully eludes predators by jumping into nearby water and then returning to the bank underwater, while the predator continues looking near the point of entry into the water. The frog is primarily nocturnal, hiding during the day in vegetation at water's edge. During summer months, it may wander some distance from water, but it stays in moist vegetation.

Reproduction   Breeding takes place year-round, and the female lays eggs in shallow water.

Mexican Burrowing Toad

Rhinophrynus dorsalis

Description   2 to 3½ inches maximum length at maturity. This highly unusual toad is the only member of the family Rhinophrynidae. It has a round body with smooth dark brown or almost black skin that appears translucent. It has a distinct light yellow or red-orange line down the center of its back, and some have similarly colored spots on the sides. The ventral surfaces are paler than the back but still relatively dark, and both the dorsal and ventral surfaces are covered with tiny light dots. The legs are quite short, and the hind legs are partially enclosed in the skin of the body. Each hind foot has a large spadelike tubercle for digging. The head is quite small, hardly more than a blunt snout protruding from the rotund body. The eyes are small and widely spaced, and the pupils are vertical. The tongue is attached at the back of the mouth, unlike that of any other toad or frog.

Voice   The call is a low-pitched guttural moan that is quite loud. Males may call from within burrows, but after heavy rains (the usual time of courtship), the males emerge from burrows to form large breeding choruses.

Range   Found in a small area of the western part of extreme South Texas.

Habitat   Within its small range in the state, it prefers low areas with soil that allows for easy burrowing, including cultivated fields and gardens.

Behavior   This nocturnal toad feeds primarily on termites or ants, and it uses its spadelike tubercles to dig into their mounds. When approached or threatened, and perhaps even during breeding calls, it inflates its body, obscuring almost entirely its small head and limbs.

Reproduction   Breeding may take place anytime after rains create sufficient pools. The female lays eggs in small clumps in the water, where they soon separate and float to the surface. The tadpoles are distinguished by what appear to be long whiskers.

Spotted Salamander

Ambystoma maculatum

Description   6 to 9¾ inches maximum head-body length. This large salamander is stout, with a long, broad head. Its unbroken, unregenerated tail is slightly shorter than the head-body length. It has small legs with 4 toes on its front feet and 5 on its back feet. It usually has 12 deep costal grooves. General coloration is shiny black to slate or bluish black. It has an irregular dorso-lateral row of round light yellow or orange spots down each side from the head to the tip of the tail. The undersides are gray.

Range   Found in the northern and central parts of East Texas.

Habitat   Like all salamanders, it requires a moist environment. It is at home in hardwood forests, near ponds in more open areas, and in temporary pools formed by flooding.

Behavior   The adults of this species are rarely seen above ground, but during spring or summer they may be found under stones or logs in moist earth. At breeding time, large numbers may gather in one pond.

Reproduction   Breeding takes place in the early spring, perhaps as early as late December, with adequate rain and warm temperatures. Courtship includes active nudging of each other. Fertilization is internal, and the female lays 1 or more egg masses with about 100 eggs each. Eggs attach to submerged vegetation, and larvae hatch in 1 to 2 months, when they are ½ inch long.

Marbled
Salamander

Ambystoma opacum

Description 3½ to 5 inches maximum head-body length. This stocky salamander has a short, broad head, a relatively short tail, and small limbs. It has 4 toes on its front feet and 5 on the rear feet. General coloration is dark gray to black on both dorsal and ventral surfaces. The smooth skin of the dorsum is patterned with variable light silvery or white markings that form broad, irregular crossbars from the snout to the tip of the tail. In some individuals, the crossbars are incomplete or fuse to surround dark spots. It usually has 11 or 12 costal grooves.

Range Found throughout East Texas, from the Red River south to the Gulf of Mexico.

Habitat This salamander may thrive in relatively dry environments, but it is always near water, such as ponds or slow-moving streams. It prefers wooded areas with swamps.

Behavior Adults of this species rarely enter the water but stay in the moist areas near sources of water.

Reproduction It breeds throughout the fall, and mates and lays its eggs on land. The female lays 50 to 200 eggs, one at a time, in a depression under vegetative debris. She curls around the eggs until the depression fills with rainwater. The eggs hatch soon after being covered with water, but hatching may be delayed until spring if there is insufficient rain to cover the eggs. The larvae are about ¾ inch long at hatching, and they transform in 4 to 6 months.

Mole Salamander

Ambystoma talpoideum

Description   3 to 4¾ inches maximum head-body length. This salamander has a large head and body and relatively short tail. Its legs are well developed but not large. It has 4 toes on its front feet and 5 on the back. The dorsal surfaces are shiny black to gray or brown, with a generous sprinkling of small bluish white flecks. There may be a pale area along the crest of the tail. The belly is gray with light blotches. There are 10 or 11 costal grooves.

Range   There are 2 separate populations, one in the central part of East Texas along the border with Louisiana and a smaller one along the Red River near the Oklahoma-Arkansas border.

Habitat   Found in lowland wooded areas, usually near floodplains, where vegetative debris provides heavy cover in a moist environment and the soft earth is suitable for burrowing. It may take advantage of mammal burrows for hiding places.

Behavior   It is a skilled burrower and spends most of its time dug in under loose earth or debris, emerging only for breeding. During the breeding season, it may migrate overland at night or during rains to nearby ponds or watercourses, where groups congregate.

Reproduction   Breeding takes place from December to February during cold weather after rains. The female deposits up to 400 eggs in numerous small masses in shallow ponds or flooded low-lying areas. The larvae may not transform until the following year.

Smallmouth Salamander
Ambystoma texanum

Description 4½ to 7 inches head-body length. It has a small head and mouth and large body. The relatively long tail may be as long as the head and body. It has strong legs, with 4 toes on the front feet and 5 on the back. It is black or dark brown top and bottom, and the dorsum is usually covered with a variable pattern of light gray speckles resembling lichen. The light markings are usually more prominent on the sides. The belly may have tiny light flecks. It has 14 or 15 costal grooves.

Range Found throughout East Texas and east-central parts of the state from the northern borders to the Gulf of Mexico.

Habitat This salamander requires abundant moisture, such as in wooded areas with swamps or in river bottoms. It may be found in cultivated farmlands near sources of water or in mammal burrows.

Behavior Nocturnal in its habits, it is particularly shy and usually remains underground or finds shelter under fallen logs or other debris near ponds or in swamps. During the breeding season, it may emerge and migrate at night or during rain to congregate in groups at nearby ponds or streams. If threatened, it may elevate its tail and wave it from side to side.

Reproduction It breeds from late January until April and deposits eggs in streams or pools. The female lays up to 700 eggs, which attach, singly or in small clutches, to underwater debris, including the undersides of rocks.

Barred Tiger Salamander

Ambystoma tigrinum mavortium

Description   6 to 12½ inches head-body length. This large salamander has a broad, somewhat flattened head with small protruding eyes. Its body is stout, and the legs are long and sturdy. It has 4 toes on the front feet and 5 on the back, with digging tubercles. The unbroken tail is usually as long as the head and body and is flattened toward the tip. The salamander has 11 to 14 costal grooves. It is elaborately patterned with yellow crossbars or spots on a black or dark brown ground. The pattern varies, but the tiger-stripe effect is common enough to give the animal its name.

Range   Found throughout the state except for the eastern third.

Habitat   It is adapted to a variety of habitats, from mountain forests to grassy plains, wherever the earth is suitable for easy burrowing. Requiring moisture, it stays near sources of water and may be found in crawfish or mammal burrows.

Behavior   It is nocturnal and spends most of its time underground or under a thick covering of debris near water. It eats earthworms and insects, as well as small mice and other amphibians. It may emerge at night or after heavy rain to feed, but it usually is abroad only for breeding, when it may crawl overland to nearby ponds or streams to congregate with large numbers of its species.

Reproduction   The breeding season usually begins in late winter after heavy rain, but breeding may take place anytime there is sufficient rain. It mates in temporary pools or still backwaters of streams where there are no fish. Egg masses attach to underwater debris, and larvae are about ⁹⁄₁₆ inch at hatching. Metamorphosis occurs at about 4 inches, but in more arid locales, larvae may reach sexual maturity without transforming and thereby remain in permanent bodies of water.

Eastern Tiger Salamander

Ambystoma tigrinum tigrinum

Description   7 to 13 inches head-body length. This large sala-mander has a broad head, small eyes, and a stout body. Its legs are long and well developed, with 4 toes on the front feet and 5 on the back. The tail is long, usually equaling the head-body length. The background color is dark brown to black, and the light markings are olive-green to yellow. The pattern created by the light markings varies from scattered spots or large blotches to crossbars, with the markings extending well down onto the sides. The belly is greenish to yellow with a marbling of darker pigment.

Range   Found throughout the eastern third of the state, from the northern borders to the Gulf of Mexico.

Habitat   An inhabitant of moist wooded areas, it may also be found in cultivated areas near ponds or streams. It must have soft earth for easy burrowing, and it may take up residence in crawfish or mammal burrows.

Behavior   It remains underground or in deep vegetative debris most of the time, but it may emerge at night after heavy rain to feed on earthworms, insects, small mice, or amphibians. It is usually abroad only for breeding, when it may crawl overland to nearby pools to congregrate with large numbers of its species.

Reproduction   The breeding season begins in late winter after heavy rain, but breeding can occur anytime there is sufficient rain. It mates in temporary pools or still backwaters of streams where there are no fish. Eggs are laid singly or in small clutches and attach to underwater debris. With sufficient rain, develop-ment is rapid, but transformation may be delayed a year if the season is dry.

Three-toed Amphiuma
Amphiuma tridactylum

Description   18 to 41¾ inches head-body length. This eellike salamander has a long body and relatively short tail. It has 4 tiny legs with 3 toes on each. It has a rounded snout and small, lidless eyes. At hatching, larvae have external gills, but those are lost during transformation, and adults retain only gill slits, one on each side of the head. There are 62 costal grooves. The dorsal surfaces are dark brown, the belly is light gray, and there is a distinct demarcation along the sides where the colors meet. There is a dark patch on the throat.

Range   Found throughout East Texas from the Oklahoma-Arkansas border to the Gulf of Mexico.

Habitat   Strictly aquatic, it is at home in the muddy waters of lakes, ponds, bayous, and irrigation ditches. It may also thrive in the shallow waters of freshwater marshes.

Behavior   The amphiuma rarely leaves the water, but it can make its way short distances on land during heavy rain. It is nocturnal, feeding at night on crawfish, earthworms, snakes, frogs, and fish. When captured, it can inflict a painful bite that will draw blood. It hibernates during the coldest weather.

Reproduction   Breeding takes place from December until June, in shallow water. Fertilization is internal, and the female lays 150 to 200 eggs in a single strand that sinks into a depression in the mud. She broods the eggs by coiling around them until they hatch. Hatchlings are about 2 inches head-body length, and they lose their gills soon after hatching.

Gulf Coast Waterdog

Necturus beyeri

Description 6¼ to 8¾ inches head-body length. This salamander remains in the larval state, reaching sexual maturity without metamorphosing. It retains its deep-red plumelike gills, but it also develops lungs. The dorsal surfaces are a rich dark brown covered by a light tan netlike pattern and numerous round or oval darker brown to black spots. The belly is lighter, and it is also covered with dark brown spots. The tail is strongly compressed laterally, and it is about the same length as the body between the front and back legs. The legs are tiny, and there are 4 toes on each foot.

Range Found in the central portion of East Texas.

Habitat Strictly aquatic, it lives in sandy-bottomed, spring-fed creeks and streams.

Behavior Little is known about the activities of this salamander. During inactive periods, it probably hides under rocks or vegetative debris along the edges of the stream.

Reproduction Breeding takes place from April to June, and fertilization is internal. The female lays 40 to 70 eggs on the stream bottom under rocks or logs. She broods the eggs until they hatch.

Southern Dusky Salamander

Desmognathus auriculatus

Description   3 to 6⅜ inches head-body length at maturity. This salamander is dark brown or black on both dorsal and ventral surfaces. On its sides, between the front and back legs and sometimes onto the tail, it has a series of white or reddish spots arranged roughly in 1 or 2 rows. The belly is marked with white speckles. The coloration and markings vary within local populations. The body is stout and the head tapers to the snout. The hind legs are larger than the forelegs, and there are 14 costal grooves along the sides between them. The tail is stout at the base and laterally compressed toward the tip, with a sharp keel on top. A groove runs from each nostril downward to the mouth. It has no lungs and breathes through the skin of its body and the lining of its mouth.

Range   Found in East Texas in the central and southern parts.

Habitat   This salamander prefers murky water with much decomposing organic matter. It is at home in swamps, stagnant ponds, river floodplains, and moist wooded areas. If its habitat dries up, it may remain in low spots under the surface crust.

Behavior   Nocturnal in its habits, it remains under vegetative debris or burrowed in the mud during the day and feeds at night. When threatened, it may leap several times its own length to avoid capture. Individuals may lighten or darken to improve camouflage.

Reproduction   It breeds from September to October and lays eggs on land under moist debris near water. The female stays with the eggs until they hatch. Hatchlings move quickly into the water and remain in the larval state until the following spring.

Cascade Caverns Salamander

Eurycea latitans

Description   2½ to 4³⁄₁₆ inches head-body length at maturity. This aquatic salamander is pale, with an indistinct darker network covering the body. Its skin is somewhat translucent, and the larger organs are visible through the skin of the belly. It may have white flecks on its sides. The body and short legs are stout, and its most distinguising characteristics are its flattened snout and dramatically sloped forehead. The eyes are medium-sized and buried in the skin. It has well-developed external gills that are faintly pigmented. It has 4 toes on the front feet and 5 on the back. There are 14 or 15 costal grooves.

Range   Found only in the subterranean water of Cascade Caverns in Kendall County.

Habitat   It thrives in the pools and streams within its small range.

Behavior   Very little is known of the habits of this cave-dweller.

Reproduction   Breeding seasons are not known. The larvae are aquatic.

San Marcos Salamander

Eurycea nana

Description   1½ to 2 inches head-body length at maturity. This small salamander is a uniform light brown with small yellowish spots arranged in a row down each side of the back. The belly is pale yellow, and the skin is translucent, revealing the larger internal organs and eggs in gravid females. The body, tail, and legs are slender. The tail is about the length of the head and body, and it has a well-developed fin. The well-developed external gills are slightly lighter-colored than the body. The medium-sized eyes are encircled with dark rings. It has 4 toes on the front feet and 5 on the back. There are 16 or 17 costal grooves.

Range   Found only in Hays County.

Habitat   It thrives in the subterranean algae growing in the spring-fed pool under San Marcos that is the source of the San Marcos River.

Behavior   Unknown.

Reproduction   Unknown.

Texas Salamander

Eurycea neotenes

Description 1⅞ to 4⅛ inches head-body length at maturity. This aquatic salamander is light brown to yellow on the dorsal surfaces, with a mottling of brown and 2 rows of light flecks down each side of its body. The lower sides and belly are cream-colored, and the skin is translucent, revealing the larger internal organs and eggs of gravid females. It has a dark bar from the eye to the nostril. The body is slender, and the legs are short and sturdy. The tail is about the same length as the head and body, and it has a narrow fin. The bright red external gills are long and well developed. The front feet have 4 toes and the back 5. There are 15 to 17 costal grooves.

Range Found in the west-central part of the state along the Balcones Escarpment in the Edwards Plateau, roughly from Williamson County west-southwest to Val Verde County.

Habitat It is at home in small subterranean streams, spring seepages, and in the headwaters of creeks.

Behavior This salamander spends most of its time under rocks and vegetative debris, but it may walk along the bottom of a stream or clear pool. Since larvae do not reach sexual maturity for 2 years and are easy prey for other species, most do not survive.

Reproduction Little is known beyond the size of the larvae at hatching, which is ⅝ inch head and body.

Dwarf Salamander
Eurycea quadridigitata

Description   2⅛ to 3½ inches head-body length at maturity. This slender salamander is yellowish brown with dark dorso-lateral stripes down each side and extending onto the tail. It may have a middorsal row of small dark spots. Color and pattern vary widely. The body and tail are slender and elongated, and the tail may be as much as 1½ times the length of the head and body. The head is small, with large protruding eyes. This species is distinguished from other *Eurycea* by having 4 toes on both front and back feet. There are 14 to 17 costal grooves.

Range   Found throughout East Texas, from the northern borders to the southeast corner and west into the east-central region.

Habitat   It is at home in flat, swampy areas, particularly in pine woods. It prefers moist terrain with a cover of pine needles and fallen logs for shelter.

Behavior   It remains in the shelter of vegetative debris most of the time, except during the breeding season.

Reproduction   Breeding takes place in the fall, and eggs are laid in the winter in shallow water. The female lays 12 to 48 eggs singly or in small clusters, and they attach to the undersides of submerged vegetative debris. The larvae hatch in 30 to 40 days and transform in the spring. They reach sexual maturity by the following fall.

Comal Blind Salamander

Eurycea tridentifera

Description   1½ to 3⅜ inches head-body length at maturity. This slender salamander is completely adapted to its subterranean, aquatic habitat. It is white to pale yellow, with pink or red external gills. It may have traces of gray pigment on the translucent skin. The larger internal organs may be visible even through the dorsal surfaces. The head is quite large, and the tiny eyes are buried in the skin. The snout is flattened, and the forehead slopes dramatically behind the eyes. The body and tail are slender, and the tail is about the same length as the head and body and has a fin. The legs are short and slender, with 4 toes on the front feet and 5 on the back. There are 11 or 12 costal grooves.

Range   Found only in Honey Creek Cave and nearby sinkhole caves on the floodplain of Cibolo Creek in Comal County and in the Elm Springs Cave of Bexar County.

Habitat   It is at home in the underground waters of limestone caves in its narrow range.

Behavior   This salamander was discovered in 1965, and its habits are still unknown.

Reproduction   Little is known except that it lays 7 to 18 eggs, and the larvae are ½ inch long at hatching.

Valdina Farms Salamander

Eurycea troglodytes

Description 2 to 3¹⁄₁₆ inches head and body at maturity. This long and slender salamander is light grayish or cream-colored, with pink or red external gills. It may have pale yellow or white lines on its sides and on top of the tail. The skin is translucent, and the larger internal organs are evident even through the dorsal surfaces. The head is large and the eyes are small and usually partially covered by skin. The forehead is almost flat. The legs are long and slender, and there are 4 toes on the front feet and 5 on the back. There are 13 to 17 costal grooves.

Range Found only in the Valdina Farms Sinkhole in northwest Medina County.

Habitat This cave-dwelling salamander lives in the subterranean pools and streams of its narrow range.

Behavior First known in 1956, little is known of its habits.

Reproduction Unknown.

Whitethroat Slimy Salamander

Plethodon glutinosus albagula

Description   4½ to 6 inches head-body length at maturity. This lungless salamander is shiny black, with a slate-colored belly and a light-colored throat. It is marked with a scattering of small silvery or white spots on its head, back, and tail and medium to large yellow spots along its sides. The body is long and slender, and the tail length is about equal to that of the head and body. The legs are relatively long and well developed. The eyes are large and protuberant. There are 16 costal grooves. The name refers to a gluelike substance that is secreted by the salamander's skin glands; it is nearly impossible to remove from one's hands.

Range   Found in south-central Texas in the eastern part of the Edwards Plateau.

Habitat   It is at home in wooded ravines and floodplains, along shale banks of rivers and streams, and at entrances to caves.

Behavior   This salamander is nocturnal and active year-round. It hides by day under rocks or rotting logs or in burrows, except during rains, when it may emerge to feed. It normally prowls only on damp nights, in search of its prey of earthworms, beetles, ants, and other insects. During hot, dry weather it becomes inactive, probably staying underground where moist conditions are maintained. It does not venture far from its immediate locale.

Reproduction   Breeding takes place during summer, and the female lays 6 to 36 eggs in a cluster underground or in damp vegetative debris in early fall. The female stays with the eggs until they hatch, and larvae emerge fully developed in October. They reach sexual maturity in 3 years.

Slimy
Salamander
Plethodon glutinosus glutinosus

Description   4½ to 8⅛ inches head-body length at maturity. This large lungless salamander is shiny black, with a slate belly. It is marked with a generous sprinkling of small silvery-white spots or brassy flecks, or both, on its head, back, and tail. The distribution of the spots and flecks is highly variable. The body is long and slender, and the tail length is about equal to that of the head and body. The legs are relatively long and well developed. The eyes are large and protuberant. There are 16 costal grooves. The name refers to a gluelike substance secreted by the salamander's skin glands; it is nearly impossible to remove from one's hands.

Range   Found in 2 locales, one in the central to south-central part of the state and the other in a small area of the northeastern part.

Habitat   This salamander needs plentiful moisture. It is at home in wooded ravines and floodplains and along the shale banks of rivers and streams.

Behavior   It is nocturnal and active year-round. It hides by day under rocks or rotting logs or in burrows, except during rains, when it may emerge to feed. It normally prowls only on damp nights in search of its invertebrate prey.

Reproduction   Breeding takes place during summer, and the female lays 6 to 36 eggs in a cluster underground or in damp vegetative debris in early fall. The female stays with the eggs until they hatch, and larvae emerge fully developed in October. They reach sexual maturity in 3 years.

Southern Redback Salamander

Plethodon serratus

Description 2½ to 5 inches head-body length at maturity. This long and slender salamander is dark gray with a light orange or red middorsal stripe extending from the top of its head down the length of its tail, narrowing at the tip. The stripe may have zigzag edges corresponding to the costal grooves. A second color phase may be dark gray with no stripe. The belly is mottled black and white. The snout is short and rounded, and the eyes are prominent. There are 18 to 21 costal grooves.

Range Found in Nacogdoches County. This salamander is poorly known in Texas. Further field work may reveal a larger range.

Habitat Strictly terrestrial, it is at home in the moist leaf litter and woodland debris of coniferous and hardwood forests.

Behavior Active primarily at night, it forages in leaf litter for its diet of invertebrates. During the day it remains hidden under debris, except during rain, when it may be seen moving about. In dry weather it burrows underground.

Reproduction Not well known.

Texas
Blind
Salamander
Typhlomolge rathbuni

Description 3¼ to 5⅜ inches head-body length at maturity. This salamander is a ghostly white to pink, with an iridescent appearance. The skin is translucent, and the larger organs are visible through the sides and belly. It has deep-red external gills. The head is large, with a strongly flattened snout and small black dots representing vestigial eyes under the skin. The body is slender, and the tail is about the same length as the head and body, tapering at the tip. The legs are quite long and spindly. The front feet have 4 toes and the back feet 5. There are 12 costal grooves.

Range Found in the Balcones Escarpment of the Edwards Plateau, mostly underneath the city of San Marcos. It is on federal and state endangered species lists, and the only entrance to its habitat, Ezell's Cave, is now a nature preserve.

Habitat It lives in the perpetual darkness of underground streams and caves in the Purgatory Creek system. It is seen above ground only when pumping or the natural outflowing of the underground waters brings it to the surface.

Behavior It is known to feed on invertebrates, such as snails, copepods, amphipods, and shrimp that live in the subterranean waters and are nourished by the droppings of bats in the caves.

Reproduction Little is known, but gravid females have been observed throughout the year. The larvae do not transform.

Blanco
Blind
Salamander

Typhlomolge robusta

Description   3⅝ to 5⅜ inches head-body length at maturity. This salamander is much like the Texas blind salamander, *Typhlomolge rathbuni,* and their distinctions are now under study. It is ghostly white to pink, with an iridescent appearance. The skin is translucent, and the larger organs are visible through the sides and belly. It has red external gills. The head is large, with a strongly flattened snout and small black dots representing vestigial eyes under the skin. Its primary differences from the Texas blind salamander are its robust, longer body and its slightly shorter and stouter legs. There are 4 toes on the front feet and 5 on the back. Its tail is broad and rounded, and it has 12 costal grooves.

Range   The range is not yet established with certainty, except that it does not occur in the same locales as the Texas blind salamander. Current data suggest that it probably is found in the Balcones aquifer to the north and east of the Blanco River.

Habitat   It lives in the perpetual darkness of underground streams and caves. It is seen above ground only when pumping or the natural outflowing of subterranean waters brings it to the surface.

Behavior   Its first formal description was in 1981, and little is known about its habits as distinct from the Texas blind salamander.

Reproduction   Unknown.

Black-spotted Newt

Notophthalmus meridionalis

Description 2⅛ to 4¼ inches head-body length at maturity. This aquatic newt is smooth-skinned but not slimy like salamanders. The adult of this species has an olive-green back and yellowish orange to orange belly, and it is covered top and bottom with many medium to large black spots. It may have uneven yellow stripes down the sides of its back, and the sides may be light blue-green. The head is large, relative to the body, and the tail is slender and usually just less than head-body length. The legs are long and well developed. The tail is vertically compressed, with a keel or fin running its length. Larvae do not transform into the land-stage eft.

Range Found in the coastal plains of South Texas, beginning about halfway down the coast and extending south to the Mexico border.

Habitat It is at home in the shallow water of quiet streams with much vegetation, in lagoons, ditches, and swampy areas. Since such habitats are not common in its limited range, it is easy to pinpoint locales.

Behavior Essentially aquatic, it seeks shelter under submerged rocks and in rocky edges of ponds. When ponds dry up, it may be forced to seek cover on land. It eats a variety of prey, including insects, leeches, worms, mollusks, and crustaceans, as well as small amphibians and their eggs. Its skin glands secrete a toxic substance that makes it unappealing to most predators.

Reproduction Breeding can take place at any time during the year, with the peak period in the spring. Up to 300 eggs are laid in shallow water and attach to submerged vegetation. Larvae appear in 3 to 4 weeks, and they transform directly into adults after about 3 months.

Central Newt

Notophthalmus viridescens louisianensis

Description 2½ to 5½ inches head-body length at maturity. The adult of this newt is yellowish brown or olive-green to dark brown above, and its belly is yellow, contrasting strongly with the back color. It has some small black spots on its back and many spots on its belly. It rarely has red spots on its sides. The head is small, relative to the body, and the body is thick. It has short legs, and the tail is vertically compressed. Larvae may or may not develop into the land-stage eft, a form they maintain for 1 to 3 years. The eft form is reddish orange and has little spotting. The size of the eft may be from 1⅜ to 3⅜ inches, with the usual size being about 3 inches, head and body. The tail of the eft is rounded.

Range Found throughout the eastern third of the state.

Habitat It is at home in shallow water in forest ponds and lakes with dense vegetation, in quiet streams, ditches, river bottoms, or swamps. The land-stage eft is at home on the forest floor.

Behavior The adult of this species is essentially aquatic, and it forages in shallow water for its prey of insects, worms, mollusks, and crustaceans, as well as small amphibians and their eggs. Its skin glands secrete a toxic substance that makes it unappealing to most predators. The eft is terrestrial, foraging on the forest floor. It is most active during or after rain showers.

Reproduction Breeding takes place in late winter to early spring. The female lays 200 to 400 eggs singly in submerged vegetation. Larvae hatch in 3 to 8 weeks at about ⅜ inch. In late summer the larvae transform either into the eft, which stays on land for 1 to 3 years before returning to the water as an adult, or directly into aquatic adults.

Western Lesser Siren

Siren intermedia nettingi

Description Record head-body length of 19¾ inches. This eel-like species is an aquatic permanent larvae that is identifiable by its 2 small legs just behind the large external gills. The feet have 4 toes each. It also has 3 gill slits on each side. The sexes are indistinguishable in color and markings, but the male is larger than the female. The dorsal surfaces are olive to dark brown or gray with a scattering of tiny black spots. The belly is dark with many light spots. Spotting may not be apparent on the darker specimens. Immature specimens may have a red band across the snout and along the side of the head. The body is long, and the head is relatively large. The small eyes are lidless. The long, slender tail is pointed at the tip and vertically compressed, with a fin running its length. Although it does have lungs, it absorbs oxygen from the water through 3 pairs of well-developed gills. It has 34 to 35 costal grooves.

Range Found throughout the eastern third of the state and south about two thirds of the way down the coastline.

Habitat This siren is at home in warm shallow waters with submerged vegetation, such as in muddy ponds, lakes, rice fields, irrigation ditches, and swamps.

Behavior Nocturnal in its habits, during the day it burrows into submerged debris or silt in shallow water. It is primarily carnivorous and forages at night for its diet of crawfish, worms, and mollusks. It may ingest some plant material along with its preferred prey. It makes a clicking sound when it is approached or surfaces for air, and it may yelp when captured. It is difficult to handle because it squirms vigorously. If its habitat dries up, it burrows into the mud and secretes a mucous cocoon that dries into a protective covering, allowing it to survive a dry spell of up to 2 months. It emerges again when rains fill its pool.

Reproduction Breeding takes place in late winter, and the female deposits about 200 eggs in early spring in a debris-covered cavity in shallow water. The larvae are about ½ inch at hatching, and they are sexually mature in 2 years.

Rio Grande Lesser Siren

Siren intermedia texana

Description Record head-body length of 27 inches. This siren is larger than the western lesser siren. The dorsal surfaces are dark gray to light or brownish gray. The lighter specimens are covered top and bottom with many small dark spots. The spots are not apparent on darker specimens. The belly is light gray, and surfaces under the 3 pairs of small external gills, the 2 small forelimbs, and around the anus are lighter than the rest of the belly. Immature specimens may have a red band across the snout and along the side of the head. The sexes are indistinguishable from each other in color and markings, but the male is larger than the female. This is an aquatic permanent larvae with a long body and relatively large head. The small eyes are lidless. The long, slender tail is pointed at the tip and vertically compressed, with a fin running its length. It has 4 toes on its 2 small forelimbs and no hind limbs. It has 36 to 38 costal grooves.

Range Found throughout the Lower Rio Grande Valley.

Habitat It is at home in warm shallow waters with submerged vegetation, such as in muddy ponds, lakes, irrigation ditches, and swamps.

Behavior Nocturnal in its habits, during the day it burrows into submerged debris or silt in shallow water. It is primarily carnivorous and forages at night for its diet of crawfish, worms, and mollusks. It may ingest some plant material along with its preferred prey. It makes a clicking sound when it is approached or surfaces for air, and it may yelp when captured. It is difficult to handle because it squirms vigorously. If its habitat dries up, it burrows into the mud and secretes a mucous cocoon that dries into a protective covering, allowing it to survive a dry spell of up to 2 months. It emerges again when rains fill its pool.

Reproduction   Breeding takes place in late winter, and the female deposits about 200 eggs in early spring in a debris-covered cavity in shallow water. The larvae are about ½ inch at hatching, and they are sexually mature in 2 years.

Reptiles
Order Chelonia: Turtles

There are 35 turtles in Texas, divided into 7 families: the marine turtles of family Cheloniidae and the leatherback of family Dermochelyidae; family Chelydridae, snapping turtles; family Emydidae, water and box turtles; family Kinosternidae, mud and musk turtles; family Testudinidae, tortoise; and family Trionychidae, softshell turtles.

Turtles are the oldest living reptiles, and their peculiar skeletons and bony shells place them among the most interesting to observe. They are found in every environment, from the ocean to the desert. All have scaly skin, and all control body temperature by behavior, so they are often seen basking. Turtles exhibit a wide variety of color and pattern, even within species, and accurate identification often requires close observation.

All turtles lay eggs, some as few as two and some as many as several hundred. All bury their eggs in cavities dug out by the female, and hatchlings must dig their way out.

Order Crocodilia: Crocodilians

There is one crocodilian native to Texas, the American alligator in the family Crocodylidae, and like its relatives elsewhere, the adult is large, and none should be approached casually. It is aquatic and carnivorous and fond of basking.

Occasionally the spectacled caiman, *Caiman crocodilus* (see photograph, plate number 32), is seen in various locales around Texas, usually in the major urban centers. It has been introduced by way of the pet trade, and specimens are sometimes released or they escape. There is no evidence at this time that they are reproducing successfully in the wild in this state.

They can be distinguished easily from the American alligator by their shelflike bony ridge between the eyes. They are otherwise relatively similar except in color, with the spectacled caiman being more gray or green-gray.

Order Squamata: Lizards

There are 61 lizards in Texas, divided into 5 families: family Anguidae, anguid lizards; family Gekkonidae, geckos; family Iguanidae, iguanid lizards; family Scincidae, skinks; and family Teiidae, whiptail lizards. None of the lizards in Texas is venomous.

The lizards of Texas vary widely in size, pattern, and color. All have scaly skin, claws on the toes (except the legless western slender glass lizard), and external ear openings. All of the natives to the state have movable eyelids, but two introduced geckos do not. The juveniles of most lizards are quite distinct from adults, so their descriptions are included in the entries.

Lizards thrive in a variety of habitats throughout the state, and all are generally diurnal. Most lay eggs, but exceptions are noted in the entries.

The tails of most lizards break off easily and then regenerate. But the regenerated tail is never as long or as perfectly formed as the original and is clearly recognizable.

Many of the lizards in Texas must be examined closely to be identified accurately. The details to look for are included in the entries.

Loggerhead Turtle

Caretta caretta

Description   31 to 48 inches maximum shell length at maturity. This turtle may weigh up to 500 pounds. The reddish brown carapace is an elongated oval tapering at the rear and with a notch over the neck. It has 3 keels that disappear with age. Older individuals show only a slight indication of a middorsal keel. It has 5 or more large scutes on the sides of the back, with the first one, usually smaller, touching the curved scute over the neck. The marginal scutes are squarish and light-colored on the edge of the shell. The plastron is creamy yellow and has 2 keels that are lost with age. The bridge between the top and bottom shells is composed of 3 or 4 large scutes not pierced by pores. The head and limbs are reddish brown above and light-colored below. The head has 2 pairs of reddish scutes on top between the eyes. It has a hooked beak that appears squarish in profile. The limbs are paddle-shaped flippers, and the front ones are larger. They have a reddish reticulated pattern over a cream color on the upper surfaces. The toes are fused. On the male, the tail usually extends well beyond the shell.

Range   Its normal range is the open seas of the Atlantic Ocean. It is sometimes seen nesting on Texas beaches.

Habitat   An ocean-dwelling turtle, it may also frequent large coastal bays. It comes ashore to nest on sandy beaches.

Behavior   A strong swimmer, it must surface occasionally to breathe air. It is omnivorous, eating a variety of marine invertebrates and plants.

Reproduction   Nesting occurs from May to August, usually during the day. A female may travel thousands of miles to nest where she was hatched. Males accompany the females to deep offshore waters, where they mate. During high tide, the female digs a nest 1½ to 2½ feet deep on a sloping beach above the waterline. She deposits up to 125 oval eggs about 1⅝ inches long. She may return several times during the season to deposit more eggs at intervals of 10 days to 6 weeks. She then does not return for 2 to 3 years. Incubation lasts 7 to 9 weeks, and hatchlings are about 1¾ inches long.

Common Green Turtle

Chelonia mydas

Description   36 to 55 inches maximum shell length at maturity. This turtle may weigh up to 650 pounds. The carapace is light and dark brown, not green, with mottling or a radiating pattern on each scute and light edges. It is a broad oval that combines a curving notch over the neck with a tapered, serrated rear to form an overall heart shape. A middorsal keel present on juveniles is completely lost with age. The 4 large scutes on the sides do not touch the curved scute over the neck. The marginal scutes are rather wide rectangles and somewhat smaller toward the rear, where they overlap slightly, creating the uneven edge. The plastron is white or yellowish, and 2 keels present on juveniles disappear. The bridge between the top and bottom shells is composed of 4 scutes. The head and limbs are olive-brown and light yellow with a reticulated pattern. The head is relatively small and flattened, with a rounded profile. There is a pair of scutes on top of the head between the eyes. The limbs are paddle-shaped flippers, and the front ones are larger. The toes are fused. On the male, the tail extends well beyond the shell and tapers at the tip to a flattened nail.

Range   Its normal range is the warmer waters of the Atlantic. It is sometimes seen nesting on Texas beaches.

Habitat   An ocean-dwelling turtle, it prefers shallow coastal waters with abundant marine plants.

Behavior   A strong swimmer, it must surface occasionally to breathe air. Its main diet is marine plants, but it may also eat invertebrates.

Reproduction Nesting occurs at night. A female may travel more than a thousand miles to nest where she was hatched. Males accompany the females to offshore waters, where they mate. The female digs a nest about 2 feet deep in the sand above the high tide line, where she deposits up to 100 spherical eggs about 1½ inches in diameter. She may return as many as 8 times in a season at intervals of 10 days to 6 weeks to dig other nests and deposit eggs. She then does not return for 2 to 4 years. Incubation lasts about 8 weeks, and hatchlings are about 2 inches long.

Atlantic Hawksbill Turtle

Eretmochelys imbricata imbricata

Description   30 to 36 inches maximum shell length at maturity. This turtle may weigh up to 280 pounds. The carapace is translucent brown and tan with a tortoiseshell mottling or radiating pattern on individual scutes. It is an elongated oval tapering at the rear with a notch over the neck. The edge is serrated toward the back of the sides and on the rear. It has a middorsal keel that is more pronounced from about the midpoint back. All of the scutes overlap. It has 4 large scutes on the side of the back that do not touch the curved scute over the neck. The marginals are rather broad rectangles overlapping dramatically at the rear, creating the uneven edge. The plastron is yellow, and 2 keels present on juveniles disappear with age. On the male it may be slightly concave. The head and limbs are yellow and brown or black with a dramatic reticulation. The head is large and has 2 pairs of dark scutes on top between the eyes. The beak is hooked like a hawk's bill, creating a squarish profile. The limbs are paddle-shaped flippers, and the front ones are larger. The toes are fused. On the male, the tail extends well beyond the shell.

Range   Its normal range is the warmer waters of the Atlantic. It is sometimes seen nesting on Texas beaches.

Habitat   An ocean-dwelling turtle, it prefers shallow coastal waters with rocky bottoms or coral reefs.

Behavior   A strong swimmer, it must surface occasionally to breathe air. It is omnivorous, eating a variety of marine invertebrates and plants.

Reproduction   Nesting occurs at night. A female may travel thousands of miles to nest where she was hatched. Males accompany the females to offshore waters, where they mate. The female digs a nest about 2 feet deep in the sand above the high tide line, where she deposits up to 200 spherical eggs about 1½ inches in diameter. She may return several times during the season to deposit more eggs at intervals of 10 days to 6 weeks. She then does not return for 2 to 3 years. Incubation lasts 7 to 9 weeks, and hatchlings are about 1¾ inches long.

Kemp's Ridley Turtle

Lepidochelys kempi

Description 23 to 29½ inches maximum shell length at maturity. This smallest of the Atlantic sea turtles may weigh more than 100 pounds. The carapace is almost circular, with small curved notches over the neck and over each of the front limbs. It has 3 longitudinal ridges and a serrated edge, which grow much less distinct with age. It is generally pale olive to gray. The middorsal scutes are small in comparison with the 5 large scutes on each side. The first scute on the side touches the curved scute over the neck. The marginal scutes are squarish on the sides and back edge, becoming wide rectangles around the front. The plastron is yellow, with 4 longitudinal ridges that are lost with age. It usually has a tiny scute at the tip of the rear. The bridge between the top and bottom shells is composed of 4 squarish scutes with a single pore on the rear margin of each. The head and limbs are light gray, and on top of the head between the eyes are 2 pairs of scutes about the same color as the carapace. The limbs are paddle-shaped flippers, and the front ones are larger. The toes are fused. On males, the tail usually extends beyond the shell. Adults may be battered or have barnacles attached to the shell.

Range Its normal range is the open seas of the warmer waters of the Atlantic and the Gulf of Mexico. It is seen on the beaches of South Texas during nesting.

Habitat A turtle of shallow coastal waters, it comes ashore to nest on sandy beaches.

Behavior A strong swimmer, it must surface occasionally to breathe air. Ridleys once gathered in huge numbers off the coast and on beaches during nesting season, but their numbers are severely reduced. It eats a varied diet of marine invertebrates, mostly crabs, and plants.

Reproduction   Nesting occurs from April to July during the day. A female may travel hundreds of miles to nest where she was hatched. Males accompany the females to offshore waters, where they mate. The female digs a nest 1½ to 2½ feet deep in the sand above the high tide line, where she deposits up to 110 spherical eggs about 1½ inches in diameter. She lays 2 or 3 clutches during a season at intervals of about 10 days. She then does not return for up to 2 years. Hatchlings are about 1½ inches long and dark gray, with light gray on the rear edge of the front flipper. The shell has prominent ridges, 3 on the carapace and 4 on the plastron.

Common Snapping Turtle

Chelydra serpentina serpentina

Description   8 to 18½ inches maximum shell length. This large turtle may weigh up to 45 pounds in the wild and much more if well fed in captivity. The color of the carapace varies from light brown to almost black, and in older individuals it may be covered with algae, obscuring the true color. The plastron is a muted yellow, and the head and limbs are dark gray on the upper surfaces and pinkish gray underneath. The carapace is oval and has 3 longitudinal keels that are serrated at the back. The keels are more prominent on young turtles. The carapace is fairly rough, but wears smoother with age. The plastron is relatively small. The head is quite large and oval, and the jaws are powerful. The eyes are visible when viewed from above. The tail is long and stout, about the length of the carapace, and it has keeled scales along its length.

Range   Found throughout the state except for the western Trans-Pecos region and the Lower Rio Grande Valley.

Habitat   It inhabits fresh water but sometimes may enter brackish waters. It prefers permanent bodies of water or slow-moving water, with soft muddy bottoms and dense underwater vegetation.

Behavior   This turtle is primarily nocturnal and spends most of its time in the water, where it is relatively docile. When on land it is quite aggressive and must be handled carefully, if at all. It can strike in any direction, including backward nearly half the length of its shell. It often buries itself in the mud in shallow water with only its eyes and nostrils above the surface. Generally omnivorous, it forages on the bottom for its diet of large amounts of aquatic plants, as well as invertebrates, fish, and carrion. It also eats waterfowl, striking from underneath and taking a heavy toll of ducklings in its habitat each year. It eats other reptiles and small mammals, too. In the coldest weather, it hibernates in the mud and aquatic vegetation, usually under an overhanging mud bank.

Reproduction   Breeding takes place from April to November, with the peak laying season in June. The female walks some distance from the water to dig a flask-shaped nest cavity 4 to 7 inches deep in moist earth. The eggs are round and white, with a hard shell, and there are usually 20 to 30 in a clutch. The size of the eggs varies from ⅕ to 1³⁄₁₀ inches. Incubation lasts 9 to 18 weeks, depending on the temperatures, and hatching may be delayed until spring by severely cold weather. The female can retain viable sperm for several years.

Alligator Snapping Turtle

Macroclemys temminckii

Description   13½ to 26 inches or more, maximum shell length. This huge turtle is the largest freshwater turtle in the country, weighing up to nearly 200 pounds. The color of the carapace is gray to brownish black, and in older individuals it may be covered with algae, obscuring the color. The plastron is quite small and gray. The head and limbs are dark brown. The carapace is oval and rough, with 3 prominent serrated keels. It has an extra row of small scutes inside the marginals on each side. The head is large and triangular, with a strongly hooked beak and powerful jaws. The eyes are low on the head and are not visible from above. The tail is long and round.

Range   Found throughout the eastern part of the state, from the northern borders to the Gulf of Mexico.

Habitat   An inhabitant of deep fresh water, it may occasionally enter brackish waters. It is most at home in deep rivers, lakes, and large streams with muddy bottoms.

Behavior   This turtle is primarily nocturnal and fairly timid. It is rarely observed on land except when females leave the water to deposit eggs. It never basks. During the day, it stays just below the surface of the water or partially buried in the mud on the bottom, surfacing frequently for air. Recent observations indicate that it may be equally at home in deep water, day or night. It is mainly carnivorous, and it is quite agile in stalking its prey, which is just about anything it can capture. In another feeding tactic, it rests on the bottom with its mouth open, exposing a pink wormlike appendage on its tongue, which it wiggles as a lure for fish. When on land it is aggressive and must be handled with extreme caution, if at all, since its powerful jaws can quickly sever fingers or hands.

Reproduction Breeding takes place from February to April. The female lays a single clutch sometime between April and June. The female walks only a short distance from the water to dig a flask-shaped nest cavity 6 to 14 inches deep in moist earth. There are usually 15 to 30 eggs in a clutch. The eggs are round and about 1½ inches across. Incubation lasts 11 to 16 weeks, depending on temperatures.

Leatherback Turtle

Dermochelys coriacea

Description   At a shell length of 50 to more than 80 inches, this is the largest of the turtles. It can weigh 600 to 1,600 pounds. The carapace is elongated, tapering almost to a point at the rear and deeply notched around the neck. It is covered with smooth skin that is slate-gray to blue-black. It has 7 prominent longitudinal ridges, 5 on the back and 1 down each side. It may have irregular patches of pinkish white, remnants of the juvenile pattern. The plastron is mostly white, with 5 longitudinal ridges. On the male, it may be somewhat concave. The head and limbs are a dark slaty color, with lighter pigment on the lips and chin and some light speckling on the neck and limbs. The limbs are paddle-shaped flippers; the front ones are larger. The toes are fused, and there are no toenails. The tail extends beyond the shell. On the male, the tail is longer than the hind limbs. Adults may be battered or have barnacles attached to the shell.

Range   Its normal range is the open seas of the warmer waters of the Atlantic. During nesting, it is seen on Texas beaches from the mouth of the Sabine River to just north of Corpus Christi.

Habitat   An ocean-dwelling turtle, it comes ashore to nest on sandy beaches.

Behavior   A strong swimmer, it must surface occasionally to breathe air. Its jaws and flippers are powerful; it uses them for protection when attacked or captured. It may also use its bellowing voice when captured or hurt. Its primary diet is jellyfish.

Reproduction   Nesting occurs from April to November late at night. A female may travel thousands of miles to nest where she was hatched. Males accompany the females to deep offshore waters, where they mate. The female digs a nest 1½ to 2½ feet deep in the sand above the high tide line, where she deposits up to 170 spherical eggs about 2½ inches in diameter. She lays several clutches during a season at intervals of 10 days to six weeks. She then does not return for 2 to 3 years. Incubation lasts 8 to 10 weeks, and hatchlings are about 3 inches long. They are black with conspicuous white patches and a covering of small, beadlike scales that are shed as they grow.

Western Painted Turtle

Chrysemys picta belli

Description 4 to 9⅞ inches maximum shell length. This turtle is intricately marked and colorful. The carapace is oval, quite smooth, and rather flat. Its color varies from olive to brown to greenish black, with each scute outlined in pale yellow or red. The rim of the shell is bordered with red, and an intricate network of light lines covers the entire surface. The shells of more mature individuals may have a covering of algae, obscuring the brilliant colors. The plastron is yellow and is marked with a large dark shape with intricate branching along the seams of the scutes. The head, neck, legs, and tail are dark green to black with fairly uniform stripes. The stripes on the head are yellow; those on the neck are red. The stripes on the legs and tail are usually greenish yellow. Females are generally larger than males. Males have long toenails on their front feet, which they use in courtship.

Range Found in 2 small locales, both in the western triangle of the state. One is in the far west tip, and the other is near the southeastern corner of New Mexico.

Habitat It prefers slow-moving shallow water with muddy bottoms, abundant underwater vegetation, and plenty of half-submerged logs for basking. It is found around the margins of lakes and in river pools, streams, ditches, and cattle tanks. No specimens have been collected recently in Texas, and suitable habitat may no longer exist.

Behavior This turtle is primarily aquatic, never more than a few feet from the water's edge. It basks in groups and is quite difficult to approach, slipping into the water at the least sign of threat. If captured, it is reluctant to emerge from its shell. Its diet is made up mostly of aquatic plants, but it also eats insects, crawfish, and small mollusks. It must be submerged to swallow its food. It hibernates early, burying itself in the mud of quiet waters, and emerges from hibernation early.

Reproduction During the nesting period, from May to July, the female digs a flask-shaped cavity 4 inches deep in moist earth near the water. She deposits 2 to 20 oval eggs, each one about 1¼ inches long. Incubation lasts 10 to 11 weeks. Hatchlings are about 1 inch, and their carapaces are keeled. An individual female may lay 2 to 4 clutches a year. Males reach sexual maturity in 2 to 5 years, females in 4 to 8 years.

Southern Painted Turtle

Chrysemys picta dorsalis

Description   4 to 6⅛ inches maximum shell length, with females usually larger than males. This turtle is intricately marked and colorful. The carapace is oval, quite smooth, and rather flat. Its color varies from olive to brown to greenish black, with each scute outlined in pale yellow or red. The rim of the shell is bordered with red, and there is a broad red or sometimes yellow stripe down the middle of the back. The plastron is yellow and unmarked. The head, neck, legs, and tail are dark green to black with fairly uniform stripes. The stripes on the head are yellow; those on the neck are red. The stripes on the legs and tail are usually greenish yellow. Males have long toenails on their front feet, which they use in courtship.

Range   Its range may include the extreme northeastern edge of the state.

Habitat   This turtle prefers shallow water with abundant underwater vegetation and plenty of basking sites. It may be in ponds, ditches, around the edges of lakes, or in the backwaters of streams.

Behavior   Primarily aquatic, it is never far from the water's edge. It basks in groups and is quite difficult to approach, slipping into the water at the least sign of threat. Its diet is mostly aquatic plants, but it also eats insects, crawfish, and small mollusks.

Reproduction   During the nesting period, from May to July, the female digs a flask-shaped cavity 4 inches deep in moist earth near the water. She deposits 2 to 20 oval eggs, about 1¼ inches long. Incubation lasts 10 to 11 weeks. Hatchlings are about 1 inch long, and their carapaces are keeled. An individual female may lay 2 to 4 clutches a year.

Western Chicken Turtle

Deirochelys reticularia miaria

Description   4 to 10 inches maximum shell length, with females larger than males. The carapace is a long, narrow oval, wider at the rear and with a smooth outline. The back is fairly high but has no keel or serrations. Carapace color varies from olive to brown, and it has a pattern of broad light lines forming a network. The rim of the shell is bordered with yellow. The yellow plastron is rigid and has dark marks along the seams of the scutes. The head is small, and the striped neck is long and limber. The combined length of the head and neck, when fully extended, is about the same as the length of the shell. The forelegs have a wide yellow stripe down the front. The hind legs are vertically striped with alternating light and dark lines on the rear surface. The tail is relatively short, with the tail of the male longer than that of the female.

Range   Found throughout the eastern third of the state.

Habitat   This turtle prefers still water, rarely entering streams or rivers. It is at home in shallow ponds, lakes, marshes, swamps, and ditches with much vegetation.

Behavior   This gregarious turtle congregates with others to bask on half-submerged logs or on land. It is shy, slipping into the water if approached. If it is encountered on land, it will retreat into its shell but will bite if intimidated. It swims easily, usually keeping its head above the water. It eats anything, but it prefers small invertebrates, worms, and dead fish.

Reproduction   One female may lay several clutches of eggs in a season. She excavates a cavity 4 inches deep and deposits 5 to 15 oval eggs, each about 1⅜ inches long. Males reach sexual maturity in 2 to 4 years at about 4 inches, females in 6 to 8 years at about 7 inches.

Cagle's Map Turtle

Graptemys caglei

Description   Females of this species are nearly twice as long as males. The shells of females are up to 6⅜ inches long, and those of males are 2¾ to 3⅝ inches long. The carapace is predominantly green. Juveniles have serrated keels with black tips, which are retained by males in maturity but not usually by females. The carapace on both sexes has cream-colored lines in whorls or small blotches within each scute. The plastron is yellow with black flecks on males. The snout is pointed, and the head is boldly striped, with a prominent light V shape on top pointing backward. The arms of the V extend downward toward the eye and curve back, forming a J. A distinctive marking is the dark-edged, cream-colored band across the chin. The legs are boldly striped with rather wide light and dark lines. Males have long toenails on the front feet, which they use in courtship.

Range   Found only in the Guadalupe River system in the southeast-central part of the state.

Habitat   It prefers pools or slow-moving stretches of the river and its tributaries. It requires adequate basking sites, such as exposed rocks, cypress knees, or half-submerged logs.

Behavior   This highly aquatic turtle rarely ventures on land except to deposit eggs. It basks on rocks or logs. Its diet is primarily insects and their larvae and aquatic invertebrates.

Reproduction   Hatchlings have been seen from September to November, which means that the breeding season is probably late spring or early summer. The female deposits 3 to 20 eggs in a cavity about 6 inches deep that she has dug in moist earth near water. The eggs are oval and about 1½ inches long. An individual may deposit 2 or 3 clutches each season.

Ouachita Map Turtle

Graptemys ouachitensis ouachitensis

Description Females of this species are nearly twice as long as males. The shells of females are 5 to 10¾ inches long, and those of males 3½ to 5¾ inches long. The oval carapace is brown, with a pattern of indistinct light oval markings surrounding darker blotches. Juveniles have a prominent, serrated keel with black spines, and the rear margins of the shell are strongly serrated. Adults retain the keel and some indications of the dark spines, but the shell becomes smooth-edged. The plastron is creamy yellow, and the intricate dark pattern of juveniles is lost or indistinct. The head is relatively small, and the large yellow spot behind each eye is squarish or rectangular. The neck is boldly striped, and 1 to 3 yellow neck stripes extend to the eye under the large spot. There is a large yellow spot under each eye and another one on each side of the lower jaw. The legs and tail are finely striped, and sexually mature males have long toenails on the front feet, which are used in courtship.

Range Found along most of the Red River's length on the northern boundary of the state.

Habitat It is at home in the river, adjacent streams, and related ponds and lakes. It must have sufficient underwater vegetation and a variety of basking sites.

Behavior This highly aquatic turtle is a gregarious basker and chooses less obvious basking sites, such as exposed roots and snags at angles to the bank, which it climbs with ease. It eats insects, crustaceans, mollusks, and aquatic plants.

Reproduction In general, members of this genus nest from May to July. The female digs a nest 6 inches deep in moist earth near the water and lays 1 to 3 clutches of 6 to 13 eggs each per season. The eggs are oval, soft-shelled, and about 1½ inches long. Hatchlings appear in the early fall.

Sabine Map Turtle

Graptemys ouachitensis sabinensis

Description Females of this species are nearly twice as long as males. The shells of females are 5 to 10¾ inches long, and those of males 3½ to 5¾ inches long. The oval carapace is brown, with a pattern of indistinct light oval markings surrounding darker blotches. Juveniles have a prominent, serrated keel with black spines, and the rear margins of the shell are serrated. Adults retain the keel and some indications of the dark spines, but the shell becomes smooth-edged. The plastron is creamy yellow, and the intricate dark pattern of juveniles is lost or indistinct. The head is relatively small, and it has a yellow oval spot behind each eye. The neck is boldly striped, and 5 to 9 neck stripes extend to the eye under the oval spot. There are yellow transverse lines on the chin. The legs and tail are finely striped, and sexually mature males have long toenails on the front feet, which are used in courtship.

Range Found in the Sabine River system in the eastern part of the state, down to the southeastern corner.

Habitat It is at home in the river and its tributaries, related ponds, and reservoirs. It must have abundant underwater vegetation and exposed roots and fallen logs on the banks.

Behavior It is a gregarious basker and chooses less obvious basking sites, such as exposed roots and snags at angles to the bank, which it climbs with ease. It eats insects, crustaceans, mollusks, and aquatic plants.

Reproduction In general, members of this genus nest from May to July. The female digs a nest 6 inches deep in moist earth near the water. She may lay 1 to 3 clutches of 6 to 13 eggs each per season. The eggs are oval, soft-shelled, and about 1½ inches long. Hatchlings appear in the early fall.

Mississippi Map Turtle

Graptemys pseudogeographica kohnii

Description   Females of this species are nearly twice as long as males. The shells of females are 6 to 10 inches long, and those of males 3½ to 5 inches long. The oval carapace is dark olive to brown, with a prominent dark brown keel. In juveniles, the keel is serrated, as is the rear margin of the carapace. Adult males may retain traces of those formations. The plastron is creamy yellow, and it may have a pattern of intricate dark lines. The head is large, especially on the female, and the neck has many fine yellow lines that do not reach the eye, being cut off by a broad yellow crescent that curves around behind the eye. There is a rounded yellow spot on the chin. The eyes are white, with black pupils. The legs and tail are finely striped, and sexually mature males have long toenails on the front feet, which are used in courtship.

Range   Found throughout the eastern third of Texas and in a band through the north-central part of the state.

Habitat   It is at home in rivers, lakes, and streams with muddy bottoms and much underwater vegetation. It requires plenty of basking sites, such as half-submerged logs and exposed rocks.

Behavior   This turtle is shy, slipping into the water at the slightest sign of approach while it is basking. It eats insects, freshwater clams, and snails, as well as aquatic plants.

Reproduction   The habits of this subspecies are not well known. In general, the turtles of this species dig flask-shaped nests about 6 inches deep in soft earth near the water. Females lay 2 or 3 clutches in a season, with 3 to 20 eggs in each. The eggs are oval and about 1½ inches long.

Texas Map Turtle

Graptemys versa

Description   This is the smallest of the map turtles, and females are just under twice as long as males. The shells of the females are 4 to 5 inches long, and those of the males 2¾ to 3½ inches long. The oval carapace is dark olive with a network of light creamy yellow lines. Each scute is distinctly convex, creating a quilted effect, especially toward the rear. The carapace is keeled, with dark-tipped, low, blunt spines. The plastron is creamy yellow with dark seams around the scutes. The head is relatively small, and it has a yellow-orange J-shaped line extending backward from the eye. That line may continue on the neck in a reddish streak. The chin is marked with a yellow or orange oval near its point and a longitudinal light blotch on each side farther back. The legs and tail are finely striped, and sexually mature males have long toenails on the front feet, which are used in courtship.

Range   Found in the Colorado River system in the center of the state.

Habitat   It is at home in the river and its tributaries and related streams and pools. It must have abundant underwater vegetation and sufficient basking sites.

Behavior   This turtle is aquatic and omnivorous. Little else is known of its habits.

Reproduction   Its reproductive habits are not known.

Texas Diamondback Terrapin

Malaclemys terrapin littoralis

Description Adult females reach a shell length of 6 to 9⅜ inches; males are 4 to 5½ inches. The carapace of this turtle is oval and prominently keeled, with the highest point toward the rear. It may have knobs along the keel. It has large scutes, each with deep concentric grooves. General coloration is light brown or gray to black. The plastron is oblong and nearly white. It is not hinged. The head and neck are nearly white with dark flecks or spots. The prominent eyes are black. The legs and tail are greenish gray and marked with many dark spots.

Range Found along the Gulf coast from the state's eastern border south to about Corpus Christi.

Habitat This turtle always remains near brackish or salt water, in the coastal marshes and lagoons and on tidal flats.

Behavior This mild-mannered turtle is an excellent swimmer and heads for the water if approached. It is also relatively agile on land and can be seen basking on mud flats. It eats crustaceans and mollusks, as well as fish and insects.

Reproduction During April and May, the female digs a nest cavity 4 to 8 inches deep in sand, where she deposits 4 to 18 eggs. The oval eggs are 1¼ inches long, pinkish white, with leathery shells. Females reach sexual maturity in about 7 years, males somewhat earlier.

Rio Grande Cooter

Pseudemys concinna gorzugi

Description *Pseudemys concinna* generally has a maximum shell length of 16⅙ inches. Females are usually 12 to 16 inches and males usually 8 to 12 inches long. The carapace of this turtle is a broad oval wider just behind the midpoint. It is fairly rough, and the marginal scutes create a sawtooth edge toward the back and at the rear. General coloration is greenish brown, with elaborate whorls created by black and yellow lines, each whorl surrounded by a broader yellow line. The undersides of the marginal scutes are marked with concentric dark and light lines around each seam. The plastron is narrow and deeply notched at the rear. It is yellow with thin dark lines along the seams. The head and neck are dark with prominent yellow stripes on top and bottom. The stripes on the side of the head curve around a distinctive oval yellow spot behind the eye.

Range Found along the Pecos River drainage system in the western part of the state and along the Rio Grande drainage system from just north of Del Rio to Brownsville. However, it is not usually seen north of the river at Brownsville. The 2 locales are separated by about 100 miles across the Trans-Pecos region.

Habitat This turtle is at home in the rivers and their more permanent related streams.

Behavior A gregarious basker, it often congregates with other species of turtles. Like other *Pseudemys* species, it is extremely wary and slips into the water at the least sign of approach.

Reproduction Turtles of the genus *Pseudemys* generally nest from late May to July. The female digs a shallow nest in sandy soil near the water and deposits up to about 20 eggs. An individual may lay several clutches in a season.

Metter's River Cooter

Pseudemys concinna metteri

Description *Pseudemys concinna* generally has a maximum shell length of 16½ inches. Females are usually 12 to 16 inches and males usually 8 to 12 inches long. The carapace of this turtle is a broad oval wider just behind the midpoint. It is fairly rough, and the marginal scutes create a reduced sawtooth edge toward the back and at the rear. General coloration is brown, with a reticulated pattern of yellow and black lines. The thin yellow lines on each marginal scute generally curve vertically around a broader yellow vertical bar in the middle of each scute. The plastron is broad and long, with a deep notch at the rear. It is yellow and has indistinct dark markings, especially toward the front, and dark lines along the seams. The head is broad and dark with many yellow lines. The lines on top of the head are wavy and converge on the snout. There are 2 other distinct yellow lines on the side of the head. One runs backward from the snout, curving over and touching the eye and back onto the neck. The other one begins at the back of the eye and runs just to the ear opening.

Range Found roughly east of a line from northwest of Dallas down to Houston.

Habitat This turtle prefers more permanent bodies of water, such as lakes and ponds with underwater vegetation and plenty of basking sites. It may also be seen in canals and large swamps and marshes.

Behavior A gregarious basker, it often congregates with other species of turtles. Like other *Pseudemys* species, it is extremely wary and slips into the water at the least sign of approach.

Reproduction Turtles of the genus *Pseudemys* generally nest from late May to July. The female digs a shallow nest in sandy soil near the water and deposits up to about 20 eggs. An individual may lay several clutches in a season.

Texas Cooter
Pseudemys texana

Description Up to 16½ inches shell length. Females are usually 12 to 16 inches and males usually 8 to 12 inches long. The low carapace is rather short, broad, and slightly rough. It is somewhat serrated at the rear. Coloration is generally dark olive-brown with yellow markings. The carapace is marked with elaborate large whorls created by thin yellow curving lines. It has wide vertical yellow lines down the center of each marginal scute and dark concentric lines on the underside of the marginal scutes encircling the seams. The plastron is yellow with tinges of red around the edge and dark seams. It may have other dark markings, especially at the rear. It has an anal notch. The head, legs, and tail are dark with many thin, light yellow lines. The head stripes are numerous, and it has a distinctive short yellow vertical bar just behind the jaw running between the stripe behind the eye and one from the mouth. The other head stripes curve upward around the bar. The short snout is somewhat pointed, and the jaw is broad and short. Sexually mature males have long toenails, which are used in courtship.

Range Found from the northwest-central part of the state in a broad area including the drainage systems of the Colorado, Brazos, and Guadalupe–San Antonio rivers and down to the coast south of Freeport.

Habitat This turtle prefers rivers, their tributary streams, and nearby ponds, with abundant underwater vegetation and plenty of basking sites.

Behavior A gregarious basker, it will often congregate with other species of turtles. It is extremely wary and slips into the water at the least sign of approach. It occasionally wanders about on land near the water's edge.

Reproduction Females lay 2 to 4 clutches of eggs during late May, June, and July in shallow nests dug near the water. Clutches contain 4 to 22 eggs about 1⅜ inches long. Incubation lasts 80 to 150 days. Females reach sexual maturity in 6 to 7 years, males in 3 years.

William W. Lamar

Dwarf American toad
Bufo americanus charlesmithi

Great Plains toad *Bufo cognatus*

Eastern green toad
Bufo debilis debilis

Terry L. Hibbitts

Western green toad
Bufo debilis insidior

Plate 1

Houston toad
Bufo houstonensis

Giant toad *Bufo marinus*

Giant toad *Bufo marinus*

Red-spotted toad
Bufo punctatus

Plate 2

Texas toad
Bufo speciosus

Gulf Coast toad
Bufo valliceps valliceps

East Texas toad *Bufo velatus*

East Texas toad *Bufo velatus*

Plate 3

Southwestern
Woodhouse's toad
Bufo woodhouseii
australis

Woodhouse's toad
Bufo woodhouseii
woodhouseii

Blanchard's cricket frog *Acris crepitans blanchardi* (left, right)

Plate 4

Northern cricket frog
Acris crepitans crepitans

Canyon treefrog *Hyla arenicolor*

Cope's gray treefrog *Hyla chrysoscelis*

Green treefrog
Hyla cinerea

Plate 5

Squirrel treefrog *Hyla squirella*   Squirrel treefrog *Hyla squirella*

Gray treefrog *Hyla versicolor*

Spotted chorus frog
Pseudacris clarkii

Plate 6

Northern spring peeper
*Pseudacris crucifer
crucifer*

Strecker's chorus frog
*Pseudacris streckeri
streckeri*

Strecker's chorus frog
*Pseudacris streckeri
streckeri*

Plate 7

Upland chorus frog
*Pseudacris triseriata
feriarum*

Mexican treefrog
Smilisca baudinii

Eastern barking frog
*Hylactophryne
augusti latrans*

Plate 8

White-lipped frog *Leptodactylus fragilis*

Rio Grande chirping frog
Syrrhophus cystignathoides campi

William W. Lamar

Spotted chirping frog
Syrrhophus guttilatus

Cliff chirping frog
Syrrhopus marnockii

Plate 9

Eastern narrowmouth toad *Gastrophryne carolinensis* (left, right)

Great Plains
narrowmouth toad
Gastrophryne olivacea

Great Plains
narrowmouth toad
Gastrophryne olivacea

Plate 10

Sheep frog
Hypopachus variolosus

Plains spadefoot
Scaphiopus bombifrons

Plains spadefoot
Scaphiopus bombifrons

Plate 11

Couch's spadefoot
Scaphiopus couchii

Hurter's spadefoot
*Scaphiopus
holbrookii hurterii*

Hurter's spadefoot
*Scaphiopus
holbrookii hurterii*

Plate 12

Southern spadefoot
Scaphiopus multiplicatus

Southern crawfish frog
Rana areolata areolata

Rio Grande leopard frog
Rana berlandieri

Plains leopard frog
Rana blairi

Plate 13

Bull frog
Rana catesbeiana

Bull frog
Rana catesbeiana

Terry L. Hibbitts

Bronze frog *Rana clamitans clamitans*

Pig frog *Rana grylio*

Plate 14

Pickerel frog *Rana palustris*

Southern leopard frog *Rana sphenocephala*

Mexican burrowing toad
Rhinophrynus dorsalis

Spotted salamander
Ambystoma maculatum

Plate 15

William W. Lamar

Marbled salamander
Ambystoma opacum

Terry L. Vandeventer

Mole salamander *Ambystoma talpoideum*

Terry L. Hibbitts

Smallmouth salamander *Ambystoma texanum*

Barred tiger
salamander
*Ambystoma
tigrinum mavortium*

Plate 16

Eastern tiger
salamander
*Ambystoma
tigrinum tigrinum*

Three-toed
amphiuma
*Amphiuma
tridactylum*

Gulf Coast
waterdog
Necturus beyeri

Plate 17

Southern dusky
salamander
*Desmognathus
auriculatus*

Cascade Caverns
salamander
Eurycea latitans

San Marcos
salamander
Eurycea nana

Texas salamander
Eurycea neotenes

Samuel S. Sweet

Samuel S. Sweet

Samuel S. Sweet

Plate 18

William W. Lamar

Dwarf salamander
*Eurycea
quadridigitata*

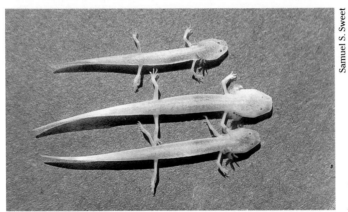

Samuel S. Sweet

Comal blind
salamander
Eurycea tridentifera

Samuel S. Sweet

Valdina Farms
salamander
Eurycea troglodytes

Plate 19

Whitethroat slimy salamander
Plethodon glutinosus albagula

Slimy salamander
Plethodon glutinosus glutinosus

Southern redback
salamander
Plethodon serratus

Texas blind
salamander
*Typhlomolge
rathbuni*

Plate 20

Black-spotted newt
Notophthalmus meridionalis

Central newt *Notophthalmus viridescens louisianensis* (left, right)

William W. Lamar

Western lesser siren
Siren intermedia nettingi

Plate 21

Rio Grande lesser siren
Siren intermedia texana

Peter C. H. Pritchard

Common green turtle *Chelonia mydas*

Peter C. H. Pritchard

Atlantic hawksbill turtle
Eretmochelys imbricata imbricata

Peter C. H. Pritchard

Kemp's Ridley turtle
Lepidochelys kempi

Plate 22

R. Andrew Odum

Common snapping turtle
*Chelydra serpentina
serpentina*

Alligator snapping turtle
Macroclemys temminckii

Peter C. H. Pritchard

Leatherback turtle
Dermochelys coriacea

Plate 23

Western painted turtle
Chrysemys picta belli

Terry L. Hibbitts

Southern painted turtle
*Chrysemys
picta dorsalis*

Terry L. Hibbitts

Western chicken turtle
*Deirochelys
reticularia miaria*

Plate 24

Cagle's map turtle *Graptemys caglei*   Cagle's map turtle *Graptemys caglei*

Terry L. Hibbitts

Ouachita map turtle
*Graptemys ouachitensis
ouachitensis*

Sabine map turtle
*Graptemys ouachitensis
sabinensis*

Plate 25

Mississippi map turtle
*Graptemys
pseudogeographica kohnii*

Mississippi map turtle
*Graptemys
pseudogeographica kohnii*

Texas map turtle
Graptemys versa

Plate 26

Texas diamondback terrapin
Malaclemys terrapin littoralis

Metter's river cooter
Pseudemys concinna metteri

Texas cooter
Pseudemys texana

Three-toed box turtle
Terrapene carolina triunguis

Plate 27

Terry L. Hibbitts

Desert box turtle
Terrapene ornata
luteola

Ornate box turtle *Terrapene ornata ornata*   Big Bend slider *Trachemys gaigeae*

Terry L. Hibbitts

Red-eared slider
Trachemys scripta
elegans

Plate 28

Yellow mud turtle
*Kinosternon flavescens
flavescens*

Mexican Plateau
mud turtle
*Kinosternon hirtipes
murrayi*

Mississippi mud turtle
*Kinosternon
subrubrum
hippocrepis*

Plate 29

Razorback musk turtle
Sternotherus carinatus

Common musk turtle
Sternotherus odoratus

Texas tortoise
Gopherus berlandieri

Plate 30

Peter C. H. Pritchard

Midland smooth softshell
Trionyx muticus muticus

Texas spiny softshell *Trionyx spiniferus emoryi*

Guadalupe spiny softshell
*Trionyx spiniferus
guadalupensis*

Peter C. H. Pritchard

Western spiny softshell
*Trionyx spiniferus
hartwegi*

Plate 31

Pallid spiny softshell
*Trionyx spiniferus
pallidus*

American alligator
*Alligator
mississippiensis*

Spectacled caiman
Caiman crocodilus

Plate 32

Texas alligator lizard
*Gerrhonotus liocephalus
infernalis*

Western slender
glass lizard
*Ophisaurus attenuatus
attenuatus*

Texas banded gecko *Coleonyx brevis*

Reticulated gecko *Coleonyx reticulatus*

Plate 33

Mediterranean gecko
Hemidactylus turcicus

Green anole
Anolis carolinensis

R. Andrew Odum

Brown anole
Anolis sagrei

Plate 34

Southwest earless lizard
Cophosaurus texanus scitulus

Texas earless lizard
Cophosaurus texanus texanus

Eastern collared lizard
*Crotaphytus collaris
collaris*

Eastern collared lizard
*Crotaphytus collaris
collaris*

Plate 35

Chihuahuan
collared lizard
*Crotaphytus collaris
fuscus*

Reticulate
collared lizard
*Crotaphytus
reticulatus*

Longnose
leopard lizard
*Gambelia wislizenii
wislizenii*

Plate 36

Northern earless lizard *Holbrookia maculata maculata* (left, right)

Keeled earless lizard
*Holbrookia propinqua
propinqua*

Texas horned lizard
Phrynosoma cornutum

Plate 37

David T. Roberts

Mountain short-horned lizard
Phrynosoma douglassii hernandesi

Roundtail horned lizard
Phrynosoma modestum

Blue spiny lizard
Sceloporus cyanogenys

Dunes sagebrush lizard
*Sceloporus graciosus
arenicolous*

Plate 38

Mesquite lizard
*Sceloporus grammicus
microlepidotus*

Twin-spotted spiny lizard
*Sceloporus magister
bimaculosus*

Big Bend canyon lizard
*Sceloporus merriami
annulatus*

Plate 39

Presidio canyon lizard *Sceloporus merriami longipunctatus* (left, right)

Merriam's canyon lizard
Sceloporus merriami merriami

William W. Lamar

Texas spiny lizard *Sceloporus olivaceus*   Texas spiny lizard *Sceloporus olivaceus*

Plate 40

Crevice spiny lizard
Sceloporus poinsettii
poinsettii

Southern prairie lizard
Sceloporus undulatus
consobrinus

Northern prairie lizard
Sceloporus undulatus
garmani

Plate 41

Northern fence lizard
*Sceloporus undulatus
hyacinthinus*

Northern fence lizard
*Sceloporus undulatus
hyacinthinus*

William W. Lamar

Rosebelly lizard
Sceloporus variabilis marmoratus

Eastern tree lizard
Urosaurus ornatus ornatus

Plate 42

Big Bend tree lizard *Urosaurus ornatus schmidti* (left, right)

Desert side-blotched lizard
Uta stansburiana stejnegeri

Southern coal skink
*Eumeces anthracinus
pluvialis*

Plate 43

Five-lined skink
Eumeces fasciatus

Five-lined skink
Eumeces fasciatus

Broadhead skink
Eumeces laticeps

William W. Lamar

Plate 44

Variable skink
*Eumeces multivirgatus
epipleurotus*

Great Plains skink *Eumeces obsoletus* (left, right)

Southern prairie skink
*Eumeces septentrionalis
obtusirostris*

Plate 45

Short-lined skink
Eumeces tetragrammus
brevilineatus

Four-lined skink
Eumeces tetragrammus
tetragrammus

Ground skink *Scincella lateralis*

Chihuahuan spotted whiptail
Cnemidophorus exsanguis

Plate 46

Texas spotted whiptail
Cnemidophorus gularis gularis

Plateau spotted whiptail
Cnemidophorus gularis septemvittatus

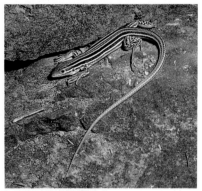

Trans-Pecos striped whiptail
Cnemidophorus inornatus heptagrammus

Laredo striped whiptail
Cnemidophorus laredoensis

Marbled whiptail
Cnemidophorus marmoratus

Plate 47

R. Andrew Odum

Six-lined racerunner
Cnemidophorus sexlineatus sexlineatus

Prairie-lined racerunner
Cnemidophorus sexlineatus viridis

Terry L. Hibbitts

Colorado
checkered whiptail
*Cnemidophorus
tesselatus*

Terry L. Hibbitts

Desert grassland
whiptail
*Cnemidophorus
uniparens*

Plate 48

Three-toed Box Turtle

Terrapene carolina triunguis

Description   4½ to 6½ inches maximum shell length at maturity. This turtle sometimes defies its name and has 4 toes instead of 3 on its hind feet. The carapace is oval and high-domed. It is usually tan or olive with large scutes on the back and small marginal scutes. The pattern of the carapace is highly variable, and rarely are 2 individuals exactly alike. It may be uniformly colored, or it may have a pattern of wide radiating lines where the light ground color invades dark smudges within each scute. It may also have light spots on the dorsal scutes. The edges of the shell curve upward in front and at the rear. The plastron is usually plain creamy yellow, but it may have dark blotches or dark rims around the scutes. It is usually about the same length as the carapace, and that of the male may have a slight depression toward the rear. It is hinged toward the front of center, and both ends are movable, enabling the turtle to close the shell tightly. The head, legs, and tail are dark olive to black, and the head and forelegs appear reddish because of a profusion of red-orange spots and blotches. The beak is slightly hooked. Males usually have red eyes and enlarged, curved toenails. Females usually have yellow eyes.

Range   Found throughout the eastern third of the state and south to about halfway down the coast.

Habitat   This is a turtle of the woodlands and dense thickets. It may also be at home on floodplains and in meadows and pastures with some moisture.

Behavior   It is terrestrial and primarily diurnal. It is most active in the early morning or after heavy rainfall. It is long-lived and may spend its whole life in a small area if conditions are right. It is mild-mannered and easily kept in suitable confines. It will learn to take food from your fingers. It normally eats earthworms and slugs, as well as wild strawberries and mushrooms poisonous to man. In captivity, it will eat berries, vegetables, and canned dog food. If alarmed, it closes its shell tightly at both ends. If conditions warrant, it can go into a dormant state in a burrow it digs.

Reproduction   The female digs a flask-shaped nest 3 to 4 inches deep during May, June, and July. She deposits 3 to 8 oval, thin-shelled eggs about 1⅜ inches long. Hatchlings usually remain in the nest through the winter. Hatchlings are brown with a light spot in the center of each dorsal scute but not on the marginal scutes. The plastron of hatchlings is not hinged. Both sexes reach sexual maturity in 5 to 7 years. The female is able to retain sperm for several years, enabling her to produce fertile eggs for several seasons after a single mating.

Desert Box Turtle

Terrapene ornata luteola

Description   4 to 5¾ inches maximum shell length at maturity. This turtle has an oval, high-domed carapace with large scutes. The ground color is olive, and it is elaborately patterned with yellow-orange lines that radiate from a central point on each dorsal scute. A distinct characteristic is the count of 11 to 14 light radiating lines on the second scute on the side. The pattern may be lost with age, creating a uniformly yellowish or horn-colored shell. The plastron is almost as long as the carapace, and it is ornately patterned with light yellow and dark radiating lines. It is hinged just forward of center, and both ends move to close the shell tightly. On the male, the plastron is slightly concave toward the rear. The head, legs, and tail are dark olive to black with yellow lines on the head and reddish spots on the front legs. The snout is square in profile, and the beak is hooked. The male has red eyes; the female has yellow eyes.

Range   Found on the far western edge of the state, more or less west of the Pecos River.

Habitat   It is at home in arid and semiarid regions, on plains, grasslands, and in pastures. It prefers open prairies with herbaceous vegetation.

Behavior   This turtle is terrestrial and primarily diurnal. It is most active in the morning and after heavy rainfall. It may burrow for protection from heat. It eats a variety of insects, including dung beetles, and also berries and carrion. Like other box turtles, it adapts easily to captivity and eats fruit, vegetables, and canned dog food. When alarmed, it closes its shell tightly at both ends.

Reproduction   The female digs a shallow flask-shaped nest in sandy soil during May, June, or the first part of July. She deposits 2 to 8 oval eggs about 1⅜ inches long and with brittle shells. Incubation lasts 60 to 70 days. Both sexes reach sexual maturity in 8 to 10 years.

Ornate Box Turtle

Terrapene ornata ornata

Description   4 to 5¾ inches maximum shell length at maturity. This turtle has a dome-shaped carapace that is somewhat flattened on top. The ground color is dark olive to black, and the ornate pattern is created by yellow lines radiating from a yellow spot on the dorsal scutes. A distinct characteristic is the count of 5 to 8 light radiating lines on the second scute on the side. The lines are in sharp contrast to the ground color, and they may be broken. The plastron is usually as long as the carapace. It is ornately patterned with dark radiating lines and smudges on a yellow ground color. It is hinged just forward of center, and both ends move, enabling the turtle to close its shell tightly. The head, legs, and tail are olive, and the snout and chin may be yellowish. It has large orange spots on its front legs. The snout is square in profile, with a hooked beak. The male usually has red eyes; the female usually has yellow eyes.

Range   Found throughout the state except along the far western edge, more or less west of the Pecos River.

Habitat   It is at home in semiarid regions, on plains, grasslands, and in pastures. It prefers sandy soil.

Behavior   This turtle is terrestrial and primarily diurnal. It is most active in the morning and after heavy rainfall. It may burrow for protection from heat. It eats a variety of insects, including dung beetles, and also berries and carrion. Like the three-toed box turtle, it adapts easily to captivity and eats fruit, vegetables, and canned dog food. When alarmed, it closes its shell tightly at both ends.

Reproduction   The female digs a shallow flask-shaped nest in sandy soil during May, June, or the first part of July. She deposits 2 to 8 oval eggs about 1⅜ inches long and with brittle shells. Incubation lasts 60 to 70 days. Both sexes reach sexual maturity in 8 to 10 years.

Big Bend Slider

Trachemys gaigeae

Description 5 to 8 inches maximum shell length at maturity. This turtle is much like the red-eared slider, but with distinct differences in color. The carapace is oval and rather flat with a weak keel and notched rear margin. It is pale olive-brown with a netlike pattern of pale orange lines. Each marginal scute has curving orange lines on the upper surface and dark blotches on the undersurface. The plastron is pale creamy orange with areas of olive, and it is marked with dark rings down the center. The head, legs, and tail are dark with many light orange stripes. The head is distinctly marked with a large orange spot on each side and a smaller orange spot just behind each eye. The lower jaw is rounded. All surfaces darken with age, but the large orange spot is usually retained. Another distinguishing characteristic is the absence of long toenails on males.

Range Found in the lower Big Bend region along the Rio Grande.

Habitat It is found in ponds and streams along the river, preferring permanent bodies of water. It may also be at home in canals, ditches, and cattle tanks near the river.

Behavior A gregarious basker, this turtle is often seen in large numbers on logs, stumps, and rocks. If the site is crowded, they may stack on top of each other. It is primarily aquatic and quite wary. Juveniles are omnivorous, but adults eat mostly aquatic plants.

Reproduction Breeding takes place from March to July. The female digs a shallow nest cavity some distance from the water and deposits the eggs during June and July. In one season the female may produce up to 3 clutches of 4 to 23 eggs each. The eggs are oval and about 1⅜ inches long. Incubation lasts 60 to 75 days, and the hatchlings are boldly and colorfully marked.

Red-eared Slider
Trachemys scripta elegans

Description 5 to 11 inches maximum shell length at maturity. This is the turtle that dime stores once commonly sold as pets. The carapace is oval and rather flat, with a weak keel and notches around the rear margin. It is dark green with light and dark markings in the form of bars, stripes, whorls, and circles, most evident in juveniles. With age, the shell darkens and markings merge. The plastron is yellow and marked with dark smudges in the middle of each scute. The head, legs, and tail are green with fine yellow stripes. The distinguishing characteristic is a broad red blotch or stripe behind each eye. The head, legs, and tail also darken with age, sometimes obscuring the red stripe. The lower jaw is rounded, and the upper jaw has a notch on each side. Sexually mature males have long toenails on the front feet, which are used in courtship.

Range Found throughout the state except in the far western triangle and along most of the border with New Mexico.

Habitat This turtle prefers quiet waters, such as slow-moving rivers and streams, swamps, or ponds. It may also be at home in lakes. It must have soft, muddy bottoms and abundant underwater vegetation.

Behavior Within its range, this is the turtle most commonly seen basking in large numbers on logs or masses of floating vegetation. In crowded sites, they will stack on top of each other as many as 3 deep. It is primarily aquatic and quite wary, slipping into the water at the least sign of approach. Juveniles are omnivorous, but adults eat mostly aquatic plants.

Reproduction Breeding takes place from March to July. The female digs a shallow nest cavity some distance from the water and deposits the eggs during June and July. In one season the female may produce up to 3 clutches of 4 to 23 eggs each. The eggs are oval and about 1⅜ inches long. Incubation lasts 60 to 75 days, and the hatchlings may spend the winter in the nest. They are boldly and colorfully marked.

Yellow
Mud
Turtle

Kinosternon flavescens flavescens

Description   4 to 6⅜ inches maximum shell length at maturity.
This turtle has a broad, rather flat, smooth carapace that is generally olive-colored, with dark-bordered scutes. The middorsal
scutes are rather small compared with the large scutes on the
sides. It usually has 23 small marginal scutes, and they are
wider than they are high, except for the ninth and tenth, which
are higher than all the others. The large plastron is yellow to
brown, with dark brown pigment along the seams. It is slightly
concave and has 2 hinges, enabling the turtle to close each end
separately. On the male, the plastron is notched at the rear. On
the female, the notch is absent or reduced. The head and neck
are olive-colored on the upper surfaces and yellow on the sides
and underneath, a characteristic evident at some distance. The
head of the male is larger than that of the female, relative to
shell size, and neither one has stripes. Both have conspicuous
barbels on the chin and smaller ones on the underside of the
neck. The legs and tail are olive. On the male, the tail is stout
and relatively long, ending in a blunt spine. The tail of the female is quite short and lacks the spine. The legs are relatively
long, and the male's rear legs have rough scale patches on the
inner surfaces.

Range   Found throughout the state, except for the eastern third.

Habitat   This turtle prefers permanent bodies of water with
muddy bottoms, such as lakes, ponds, and cattle tanks. It may
also be found in slow-moving water, such as canals and ditches.

Behavior   A primarily aquatic, bottom-dwelling turtle, it may be
on land during heavy rain, for early morning foraging, or for
nesting. It usually basks in shallow water with the top of the
shell exposed. If its habitat dries up, it will cross overland to find
another body of water. It eats aquatic invertebrates, worms, and
tadpoles. When picked up or otherwise alarmed, it secretes

a smelly substance from musk glands on the sides. It may burrow under vegetative debris or in the mud during the coldest months.

Reproduction   In June the female digs a shallow nest using her forelegs. She deposits 1 to 6 eggs that are oval and hard-shelled. Both male and female reach sexual maturity in 6 to 7 years.

Mexican Plateau Mud Turtle

Kinosternon hirtipes murrayi

Description 3¾ to 6⅝ inches maximum shell length at maturity. This turtle's elongated oval shell is somewhat arched and has a low keel. It is olive-brown to nearly black, with dark pigment along the seams. The middorsal scutes are rather small compared with the large scutes on the sides. It usually has 23 small marginal scutes, and they are wider than they are high, except for the tenth, which is higher than all the others. The large plastron is yellowish to brown, with dark pigment along the seams. It is slightly concave and has 2 hinges, enabling the turtle to close each end separately. On the male, the plastron is notched at the rear. On the female, the notch is absent or reduced. The head and neck are dark olive to dark brown, with many small dark spots and streaks. The head of the male is larger than that of the female, relative to shell size. Both usually have a pair of conspicuous barbels on the chin and none on the neck. The legs and tail are dark. On the male, the tail is stout and relatively long, ending in a blunt spine. The tail of the female is quite short and without the spine. The legs are relatively long, and the male's rear legs have rough scale patches on the inner surfaces.

Range Found in a small locale in the western part of the Big Bend region.

Habitat This turtle is at home in slow-moving streams and backwaters of the Rio Grande, as well as in nearby ponds, lakes, and cattle tanks.

Behavior A primarily aquatic, bottom-dwelling turtle, it is most active at night. It may bask in shallow water with the top of the shell exposed. It forages at night for aquatic invertebrates, worms, and tadpoles. When picked up or otherwise alarmed, it secretes a smelly substance from musk glands on the sides.

Reproduction The reproductive habits of this turtle are not known, except that it probably nests in June, laying 4 to 7 eggs.

Mississippi Mud Turtle

Kinosternon subrubrum hippocrepis

Description 3 to 4⅞ inches maximum shell length at maturity. This turtle has an elongated oval shell that is smooth and slightly arched. It is uniformly olive to dark brown to almost black. The middorsal scutes are small relative to the large scutes on the sides. It usually has 23 small marginal scutes, much wider than they are high and all about the same size. The plastron is yellowish brown, and it may have some dark brown markings. It is slightly concave and has 2 hinges, enabling the turtle to close each end separately. On the male, the plastron is notched at the rear. On the female, the notch is absent or reduced. There is a wide bridge between the upper and lower shells at about the midpoint of the sides. The head and neck are dark olive to almost black, and the head is marked with 2 light yellow stripes on each side. The snout is rather pointed and appears square in profile. The head of the male is larger than that of the female, relative to shell size. Both have conspicuous barbels on the chin and smaller ones on the underside of the neck. The legs and tail are dark olive to almost black. On the male, the tail is stout and relatively long, ending in a blunt spine. The tail of the female is quite short and usually without the spine. The legs are relatively long, and the male's rear legs have rough scale patches on the inner surfaces.

Range Found throughout the eastern side of the state and south along the coast to below Corpus Christi.

Habitat Able to tolerate brackish water, this turtle prefers shallow slow-moving water with soft, muddy bottoms and abundant aquatic plants. It is at home in bayous, swamps, lagoons, ditches, and small ponds.

Behavior A primarily aquatic, bottom-dwelling turtle, it may be on land during heavy rain, for early morning foraging, or for nesting. It usually basks in shallow water, with the top of its shell exposed. When picked up or otherwise alarmed, it secretes a smelly substance from musk glands on the sides. It may burrow under vegetative debris or in the mud during the coldest months.

Reproduction   Breeding usually takes place from mid-March to May. During June, the female digs a shallow nest in sandy soil or vegetative debris, and in it she deposits 1 to 6 oval eggs about 1 inch long with hard shells. An individual can produce several clutches in a season, which can begin as early as October.

Razor-backed Musk Turtle

Sternotherus carinatus

Description   4 to 5⅞ inches maximum shell length at maturity. This distinctive turtle has a prominently keeled carapace, with slightly overlapping scutes. At the midpoint of the back, the shell is about half as high as it is wide. It is generally light-colored, usually a light orange-brown, with small dark spots or streaks and dark pigment along the seams. The dark markings may disappear with age. The middorsal scutes are small relative to the large scutes on the sides. It usually has 23 small marginal scutes, all the same size when whole, but often some are eroded by combat or by algae or fungi attacks on damaged tissue. The plastron is small and has a single hinge to the front of center. It has only 10 scutes, lacking the one near the throat. It is yellow with some dark brown smudges. The head and neck are light, with many small dark spots and speckles. The snout is rather pointed and tubular. Both sexes have barbels on the chin only. The legs and tail are light and have many small dark spots. On the male, the tail is stout and relatively long, ending in a blunt spine. The tail of the female is quite short and lacks the spine. The legs are relatively long, and the male's rear legs have rough scale patches on the inner surfaces.

Range   Found throughout East Texas and across into the north-central region.

Habitat   This turtle prefers slow-moving streams and swamps adjacent to rivers. It requires a soft, muddy bottom and abundant aquatic plants.

Behavior   A primarily aquatic, bottom-dwelling turtle, it basks more than other musk turtles, usually in shallow water with the top of its shell exposed. It may burrow in mud during the coldest months. It is capable of secreting a smelly musk from glands on its sides, but it usually does not, even when picked up. In an ideal habitat, the number of individuals may be quite large.

Reproduction   The reproductive habits of this turtle are not well known.

Common Musk Turtle

Sternotherus odoratus

Description   3 to 5⅜ inches maximum shell length at maturity. This turtle has a smooth, oval, high-domed carapace that is dull brown to black and usually caked with mud and algae. The outline is somewhat elongated and narrower toward the front. The middorsal scutes are rather small compared with the large scutes on the sides. It usually has 23 small marginal scutes that are much wider than they are high. The distinctive plastron is small, with 11 scutes and a single hinge toward the front. The yellow scutes are widely spaced, with soft, white areas between. The scutes are more widely spaced on the male than on the female. The head and neck are dark olive to black, and 2 light yellow lines on each side run from the pointed snout backward onto the neck, 1 above and 1 below the eye. The neck is quite long. The head of the male is larger than that of the female, relative to shell size. Both sexes have barbels on both the chin and the underside of the neck. The legs and tail are a dark olive color. On the male, the tail is stout and relatively long, ending in a blunt spine. The tail of the female is short and usually lacks the spine. The legs are relatively long, and the male's rear legs have patches of tilted scales on the inner surfaces.

Range   Found throughout East Texas and most of the center of the state, including about halfway down the coast.

Habitat   It may be found in almost any permanent body of water in its range, as well as in slow-moving shallow streams with muddy bottoms.

Behavior   A highly aquatic, bottom-dwelling turtle, it basks in shallow water with the top of its shell exposed. It is rarely on land except for nesting, but it may climb slanting tree trunks at the water's edge to get a better basking site. It forages on the bottom for its varied diet. The male is especially aggressive, and when picked up, it will almost always secrete a smelly substance from musk glands on its sides. It may also attempt to bite, and with its long neck it can reach back over its shell or around the sides.

Reproduction   These turtles mate underwater, and the female uses her forelegs to dig a shallow nest under rotting logs at the water's edge. Up to 9 eggs are deposited sometime from February to June. They are off-white with a pure white band and thick oval shells about 1⅛ inches long. Incubation lasts 60 to 84 days.

Texas Tortoise

Gopherus berlandieri

Description 4½ to 8¾ inches maximum shell length at maturity. This distinctive turtle has a broad, domed carapace that varies in color from tan to brown. The scutes on the back and sides are about the same size, and the marginal scutes are large, almost twice as high as they are wide. The marginal scutes overlap slightly, creating a jagged edge, especially toward the rear. Those around the front of the shell turn upward slightly. The front edge is deeply notched around the neck. The scutes on the top of the shell are grooved with fine concentric growth rings in squarish rather than rounded formations. The grooves may surround lighter yellowish centers. The yellow plastron is not hinged, and it may be elongated in front, forked, and upward curving, especially in adult males. On males it is slightly concave. The bridge between the top and bottom shells is well developed, and there are usually 2 axillary scutes. The head, legs, and tail are gray. The head is wedge-shaped, and the snout is somewhat pointed. It appears squarish in profile. The front legs are larger than the back legs, and they are flattened and heavily scaled. The back legs are round and stumpy, like elephants' feet.

Range Found throughout the southern part of the state.

Habitat It is well adapted to arid regions and at home on sandy soil with sparse, low vegetation.

Behavior This terrestrial turtle is most active early in the morning or late in the afternoon. It is capable of burrowing in the sand, but it usually creates resting places by scraping out a shallow depression under a bush or at the base of a clump of cactus. It may enter burrows dug by other animals. When alarmed, it folds its heavily armored, flattened forelegs to close the front opening of the shell. It is primarily vegetarian, preferring the pads, fruit, and flowers of the prickly pear cactus. It also eats grass and the stems and leaves of other low-growing plants. It can go without water for long periods, taking moisture from its diet.

Reproduction Nesting occurs from April to September. The female digs several shallow nests under low bushes and usually deposits 1 egg in each, up to 7 eggs total. The hard-shelled eggs are oval and about 1½ inches long. Both sexes reach sexual maturity in 3 to 5 years.

Midland Smooth Softshell

Trionyx muticus muticus

Description The female grows to nearly twice the size of the male. The shells of adult females are 7 to 14 inches long; those of adult males are 5 to 7 inches long. The carapace is almost round and covered with a soft leathery skin. It is uniformly orange-brown to olive and may have irregular darker markings. It is completely smooth, lacking the sandpaperlike texture of other softshells. The edges of the carapace bend easily. The hint of the skeleton underneath may show through the shell on top and bottom. The plastron is white or gray and unmarked. Its size is reduced toward the rear. The head, legs, and tail are about the same color as the carapace. The snout is long and tubular, with the nostrils on the tip. The nostrils lack the interior ridge present in other softshells. Pale stripes on the head include one on each side of the snout and another, more prominent and with black borders, from behind the eye onto the neck. The legs and feet are not patterned. The broad, flat feet are fully webbed and have 3 toenails on each. The tail of the male is much longer than that of the female, extending well beyond the carapace. The tail of the female barely reaches the edge of the shell. On both sexes, the anus is near the tip of the tail, rather than at its base.

Range Found in all of the eastern side of the state, to about halfway down the coast, and in a narrow horizontal band across the middle of the Panhandle.

Habitat Primarily a turtle of rivers and larger streams, it prefers a moderate to fast current and sandy or muddy bottoms. It may also inhabit creeks and smaller streams, but usually not lakes.

Behavior A highly aquatic turtle, it often basks in shallow water, sometimes under a thin layer of sand or mud, with its long neck stretched to expose its nostrils for breathing. It may bask on a sandy bank, but with ready access to the water, where it retreats quickly when alarmed. It is a strong and fast swimmer and can catch fish and frogs. Its primary diet, however, is crawfish and other small invertebrates. Handle only with caution, because it is aggressive, and its long neck enables it to reach over and under its shell with ease.

Reproduction   Nesting occurs from May to July. The female uses her hind feet to dig a nest cavity 6 to 9 inches deep in a sandbank. She deposits up to 33 hard-shelled, spherical eggs about ⅞ inch in diameter. Incubation lasts 8 to 10 weeks.

Texas Spiny Softshell

Trionyx spiniferus emoryi

Description   The female grows to nearly twice the size of the male. The shells of adult females are 7 to 17 inches long; those of adult males are 5 to 9 inches long. The carapace is oval, broader and rounded at the rear, with a small rounded projection over the neck. It is covered with a soft leathery skin and is distinctly marked. It is generally olive to tan with a light border around the edge that is much wider at the rear. The light border may be rimmed inside with a narrow dark line. It has small dark-bordered light spots over the rear third of the carapace. Females tend to lose the light spots with age, becoming mottled. The carapace of both sexes is textured with many tiny spines, creating a sandpaper effect to the touch. The texture is less pronounced in females. A hint of the skeleton underneath may show through the shell top and bottom. The plastron is white or gray, unmarked, and smaller toward the rear. The upper surfaces of the head, neck, legs, and tail are about the same color as the carapace and almost white underneath. The upper surfaces are covered with a profusion of small black flecks and spots. The snout is long and tubular, with nostrils on the tip. The nostrils are ridged inside. On each side of the head are 2 dark-bordered light lines. The broad, flat feet are fully webbed and have 3 toenails on each. The tail of the male is much longer than that of the female, extending well beyond the carapace. The tail of the female barely reaches the edge of the shell. On both sexes, the anus is near the tip of the tail, rather than at its base.

Range   Found along the drainages of the Rio Grande and Pecos rivers and throughout the Lower Rio Grande Valley.

Habitat   A resident of mainly permanent rivers and streams, it prefers a moderate to fast current and sandy or muddy bottoms. It may also be in lakes adjacent to the rivers.

Behavior A highly aquatic turtle, it often basks in shallow water, sometimes under a thin layer of sand or mud, with its long neck stretched to expose its nostrils for breathing. It may bask on a sandy bank, logs, or floating debris, but it always has quick access to water, where it retreats with great speed when alarmed. It is a strong and fast swimmer and apparently quite long-lived. It is carnivorous, preferring crawfish, frogs, fish, and small invertebrates. When its watercourse dries up, it may bury itself in mud, waiting for rains to restore the current. Handle only with caution, because it is aggressive, and its long neck enables it to reach over and under its shell with ease.

Reproduction Nesting occurs from May to August. The female uses her hind feet to dig a nest cavity 6 to 9 inches deep in a sandbank in the sun. She deposits up to 32 hard-shelled, spherical eggs about 1⅛ inches in diameter. An individual may deposit more than one clutch a season. Hatchlings appear from late August to October or remain in the nest until the following spring.

Guadalupe Spiny Softshell

Trionyx spiniferus guadalupensis

Description The female grows to nearly twice the size of the male. The shells of adult females are 7 to 17 inches long; those of adult males are 5 to 9 inches long. The carapace is oval, broader and rounded at the rear, with a small rounded projection over the neck. It is covered with a soft leathery skin that is generally olive to tan with many small black-bordered light spots over the entire surface of the carapace. Females tend to lose the light spots with age, becoming mottled. The carapace is rimmed with a light border that is somewhat wider at the rear. The light border may be rimmed inside with a narrow dark line. The carapace of both sexes is textured with many tiny spines, creating a sandpaper effect to the touch. The texture is less pronounced in females. A hint of the skeleton underneath may show through the shell on top and bottom. The plastron is white or gray, unmarked, and smaller toward the rear. The upper surfaces of the head, neck, legs, and tail are about the same color as the carapace and almost white underneath. The upper surfaces are covered with a profusion of small black flecks and spots. The snout is long and tubular, with nostrils on the tip. The nostrils are ridged inside. On each side of the head are 2 dark-bordered light lines. The broad, flat feet are fully webbed and have 3 toenails on each. The tail of the male is much longer than that of the female, extending well beyond the carapace. The tail of the female barely reaches the edge of the shell. On both sexes, the anus is near the tip of the tail, rather than at its base.

Range Found in the south-central part of the state, extending southeast down to the coast in the drainage systems of the Guadalupe–San Antonio and Nueces rivers.

Habitat A resident of rivers and larger streams, it prefers a moderate to fast current and sandy or muddy bottoms. It may also inhabit smaller streams or lakes and ponds adjacent to the rivers.

Behavior A highly aquatic turtle, it often basks in shallow water, sometimes under a thin layer of sand or mud, with its long neck stretched to expose its nostrils for breathing. It may bask on a sandy bank, logs, or floating debris, but it always has quick access to water, where it retreats with great speed when alarmed. It is a strong and fast swimmer and apparently quite long-lived. It is carnivorous, preferring crawfish, frogs, fish, and small invertebrates. Handle only with caution, because it is aggressive, and its long neck enables it to reach over and under its shell with ease.

Reproduction Nesting occurs from May to August. The female uses her hind feet to dig a nest cavity 6 to 9 inches deep in a sandbank, where she deposits up to 32 hard-shelled, spherical eggs about 1⅛ inches in diameter. An individual may deposit more than one clutch a season.

Western Spiny Softshell

Trionyx spiniferus hartwegi

Description   The female grows to more than twice the size of the male. The shells of adult females are 7 to 17 inches long; those of adult males are 5 to 7¼ inches long. The carapace is oval, broader and rounded at the rear, with a small rounded projection over the neck. It is covered with a soft leathery skin that is generally olive-gray to yellowish brown, with many small black-bordered light spots over the entire surface of the carapace. The spots may be a little larger in the center of the shell. Females tend to lose the light spots with age, becoming mottled. The carapace is rimmed with a light border that is somewhat wider at the rear. The light border may be rimmed inside with a narrow dark line. The carapace of both sexes is textured with many tiny spines, creating a sandpaper effect to the touch. The texture is less pronounced in females. A hint of the skeleton underneath may show through the shell on top and bottom. The plastron is white or gray, unmarked, and smaller toward the rear. The upper surfaces of the head, neck, legs, and tail are about the same color as the carapace and almost white underneath. The upper surfaces are covered with a profusion of small black flecks and spots, especially on the feet. The snout is long and tubular, with nostrils on the tip. The nostrils are ridged inside. On each side of the head are 2 dark-bordered light lines. The broad, flat feet are fully webbed and have 3 toenails each. The tail of the male is much longer than that of the female, extending well beyond the carapace. The tail of the female barely reaches the edge of the shell. On both sexes, the anus is near the tip of the tail, rather than at its base.

Range   Found in a broad band across the upper Panhandle, extending to the northern boundary only on the eastern side.

Habitat   Found in rivers and related drainage systems with swift currents and sandy or muddy bottoms.

Behavior A highly aquatic turtle, it often basks in shallow water, sometimes under a thin layer of sand or mud, with its long neck stretched to expose its nostrils for breathing. It may bask on a sandy bank, logs, or floating debris, but it always has quick access to water, where it retreats with great speed when alarmed. It is a strong and fast swimmer and apparently quite long-lived. It is carnivorous, preferring crawfish, frogs, fish, and small invertebrates. Handle only with caution, because it is aggressive, and its long neck enables it to reach over and under its shell with ease.

Reproduction Nesting occurs from May to August. The female uses her hind feet to dig a nest cavity 6 to 9 inches deep in a sandbank, where she deposits up to 32 hard-shelled, spherical eggs about 1⅛ inches in diameter. An individual may deposit more than one clutch a season.

Pallid Spiny Softshell

Trionyx spiniferus pallidus

Description   The female grows to about twice the size of the male. The shells of adult females are 7 to 16½ inches long; those of adult males are 5 to 8½ inches long. This turtle is a paler version of the other softshells. Its carapace is a broad oval with a small rounded projection over the neck. It is covered with a soft leathery skin that is pale olive with small white spots on the rear half. The spots do not have dark borders. The carapace is rimmed by a light border somewhat wider at the rear, and the light border may be rimmed inside by a dark line. The carapace is textured with many tiny spines, creating a sandpaper effect more prominent on the male. A hint of the skeleton underneath may show through the shell on top and bottom. The plastron is white, unmarked, and smaller toward the rear. The upper surfaces of the head, neck, legs, and tail are about the same color as the carapace and white underneath. The upper surfaces are covered with a profusion of small black flecks and spots. The snout is long and tubular, with nostrils on the tip. The nostrils are ridged inside. On each side of the head are 2 dark-bordered light lines. The broad, flat feet are fully webbed and have 3 toenails each. The tail of the male is much longer than that of the female, extending well beyond the carapace. The tail of the female barely reaches the edge of the shell. On both sexes, the anus is near the tip of the tail, rather than at its base.

Range   Found in most of the northern and eastern part of the state, south to about the midpoint on the coast, west into the west-central region, and north into the lower Panhandle.

Habitat   A resident of rivers and larger streams, it prefers a moderate to fast current and sandy or muddy bottoms. It may also inhabit smaller streams or lakes and ponds adjacent to the rivers.

Behavior   A highly aquatic turtle, if often basks in shallow water, sometimes under a thin layer of sand or mud, with its long neck stretched to expose its nostrils for breathing. It may bask on a sandy bank with ready access to water, where it retreats quickly when alarmed. It is a strong and fast swimmer that catches fish and frogs. It also eats crawfish and other small invertebrates.

Reproduction   Nesting occurs from May to August. The female digs a nest cavity 6 to 9 inches deep in a sandbank, where she deposits up to 32 hard-shelled, spherical eggs about 1⅛ inches in diameter. An individual may deposit more than one clutch a season.

American Alligator

Alligator mississippiensis

Description   The largest reptile in North America, adults are 6 to 16 feet and may grow to more than 19 feet long. Males generally are larger than females. It is distinguished from the American crocodile by its broad rounded snout. Unlike the crocodile, when the mouth of the alligator is closed, the enlarged fourth tooth in the lower jaw fits into a socket in the upper jaw, as do the other teeth. It is generally very dark, appearing black. Some adults may retain vague light crossbars, which are bright yellow on black in juveniles. The dorsal scales are laid over bony plates, and several longitudinal rows are dramatically keeled. The scales on the sides are small and soft. The ventral scales are large, soft, and rectangular. The scales on the long tail are keeled down each side of the top, and the 2 rows merge to form 1 strong keel down the middle at about the midpoint on the tail. The head is large and dominated by the long jaws. The eyes and nostrils protrude, enabling it to remain submerged while breathing and keeping watch. Valves on the nostrils and ear openings can be closed when the animal is underwater. The legs are rather long and stout. The front feet have 5 toes, and the hind feet are webbed and have 4 toes. The tail is usually at least as long as the head and body. It is heavily muscled, quite flexible, and strong.

Range   Found throughout the eastern and east-central part of the state most of the way down the coast and in the extreme southern tip.

Habitat   It is found in river swamps, lakes, and bayous, and it can tolerate the brackish water of coastal marshes.

Behavior   The alligator is semiaquatic, spending much of its time basking on land, always near water. It is a strong and agile swimmer, often cruising through the water with only its eyes and nostrils showing. It digs deep holes in the mud along the banks where it hibernates during the coldest months or takes refuge in a dry season. It is carnivorous and eats most anything in its habitat, including fish, lizards, snakes, small mammals, and waterfowl, as well as crustaceans. When it captures a larger animal, it will twist underwater until the animal drowns. It can chew underwater with the aid of a valve at the back of the tongue, which closes off the throat, but it must surface to swallow. The alligator can be noisy, with different voices at different ages. The voice of a juvenile is a high-pitched yip or a low moaning grunt. That of the adult male is a deep throaty roar, which can be heard at great distances. The adult female also produces a bellowing roar, but not as loud, and she uses a grunting sound to call her young to her side. All ages can produce a hissing sound.

Reproduction The calls of adults are most commonly heard during breeding season, which begins soon after they emerge from hibernation between early April and early May. In June, the female builds a large mound, about 6 feet across and 2 or 3 feet high, of mud and leaves. She excavates the center, where she deposits up to 60 hard-shell, oval eggs about 3 inches long. She then covers over the egg chamber. During the incubation period of about 9 weeks, she stays near the mound, and when she hears the hatchlings calling, she scratches the chamber open to let them out. Hatchlings are about 9 inches long, and they stay with the female for a year or more. She may be aggressively protective of her brood.

Texas Alligator Lizard

Gerrhonotus liocephalus infernalis

Description   10 to 20 inches from snout to tip of long tail, which may be almost twice the length of the head and body. This rather stiff, elongated lizard has the hard platelike scales characteristic of the Anguid family, as well as the deep fold along each side, which permits flexibility for breathing and eating and to accommodate eggs. It has small, weak legs and a strong tail, which it may use in a prehensile manner. It will shed its tail if necessary and regenerate a new one. It has yellow eyes with closable eyelids and obvious external ear openings. Coloration varies from dull yellow to reddish brown on the dorsal surfaces, with irregular light- and dark-flecked crossbands on the back and onto the tail. The head is usually paler, and both head and legs are unmarked. The ventral surfaces are pale gray and the belly may have dark marks.

Range   Found from the Edwards Plateau region through the Big Bend region.

Habitat   This mainly terrestrial lizard is usually found on rocky hillsides with low-growing vegetation.

Behavior   Slow and deliberate, this diurnal lizard may inflate itself when annoyed. It is carnivorous, feeding on many insects and spiders, as well as small rodents, snakes, and lizards.

Reproduction   This lizard breeds throughout the year, and the female broods the eggs during incubation. The young are more distinctly marked than adults, with light, narrow crossbands on dark brown or black dorsal surfaces. They are about 4 inches at hatching.

Western Slender Glass Lizard

Ophisaurus attenuatus attenuatus

Description 22 to 42 inches from snout to tip of tail, with tail usually just under 2½ times the length of head and body. The only legless lizard in Texas, this lizard is commonly referred to as a glass snake and is often mistaken for a snake at first glance. It can be distinguished as the lizard it is by its closable eyelids and obvious ear openings. Its platelike scales make its movements stiff, and it has a deep groove along each side, a characteristic of the Anguid family. Coloration is pale yellow with a prominent dark middorsal stripe and dark stripes or dark speckles below the lateral grooves. White flecks in the center of the back scales become more obvious with age, and longitudinal stripes may fade.

Range Found throughout the eastern half of the state, including the eastern half of the southern tip.

Habitat This terrestrial lizard inhabits dry grasslands and dry wooded areas.

Behavior Believed to be abundant in its range, this diurnal lizard is rarely seen. It usually burrows only for hibernation, and its diet is varied, including insects, small mammals, and other lizards. The word "glass" in its name refers to its ability to shatter its tail into many pieces when threatened. In folklore, this animal is said to return to its shattered tail at night to piece itself together again. In reality, a new tail is regenerated on the body after several weeks, but it is never as long as the original tail.

Reproduction Mating occurs in spring, and the female broods eggs during incubation. Hatchlings are distinctly marked and are about 5 inches long.

Texas Banded Gecko

Coleonyx brevis

Description   4 to 4¾ inches from snout to tip of tail at maturity. The tail is usually about the same length as head and body. Females tend to be larger than males. The slender body, with relatively large head and thick tail, is crossed by bands of brown alternating with narrower creamy yellow to pinkish spaces. With age, the bands are interrupted by pale blotches, and both bands and spaces produce dark brown spots, creating a mottled look at maturity, although the bands may be visible. The small, equal-sized legs are light pinkish brown. The tail is fragile and easily lost, and regeneration occurs. Regenerated tails are seldom as long as originals. Distinguishing characteristics include slender toes without pads; skin with small delicate granular scales; large eyes trimmed in pale yellow or white, with vertical pupils and movable eyelids.

Range   Common wherever its preferred habitat exists throughout southwestern Texas, including the western part of South Texas.

Habitat   This gecko inhabits rocky desert areas and canyons near level ground. Not a good climber, it seeks shelter by day under surface rocks, in rock outcroppings or crevices, or under plant debris.

Behavior   It is terrestrial and remains under cover during the day, becoming active at dusk. After dark it forages for insects and small spiders, usually on level ground, and may wander several yards from rocky hiding places. It can be seen on roadways at night. When alarmed it may curl its tail over its back, swaying the tail from side to side, and has often been observed running with the tail elevated, scorpion-style. It emits faint squeaks when molested and possibly when it is signaling territorial claims and during breeding.

Reproduction   This gecko's habits are not well known. Breeding probably takes place during 3 to 5 months beginning in April. Clutches contain 1 or 2 smooth white eggs, and hatchlings are about 1¾ inches long.

Reticulated Gecko

Coleonyx reticulatus

Description 5½ to 6⅝ inches from snout to tip of tail. As a juvenile, this gecko resembles the Texas banded gecko, with dark brown crossbands separated by narrower light-colored spaces. However, it grows up to 37 percent larger, has dorsal rows of enlarged tubercles that create texture on the otherwise smooth fine-scaled skin, and appears quite pink overall. At maturity, the bands may disappear altogether, leaving a pattern of brown spots on the pink body. Other distinguishing characteristics include slender toes without pads, large eyes with vertical pupils, and prominent movable eyelids.

Range Discovered in the mid-fifties, this gecko is found in the Big Bend region, in Brewster and Presidio counties. It is not commonly seen.

Habitat Found in rocky desert areas where it can find convenient shelter during daylight.

Behavior The behavior of this terrestrial and nocturnal gecko is not well known. Like the Texas banded gecko, it may squeak when captured or disturbed. It is most often seen on roadways on cool summer nights, after daytime rains. It is usually observed carrying its tail elevated over its back.

Reproduction Not well known. In captivity it has been reported to deposit clutches of 2 eggs in July.

Bent-toed Gecko
Cyrtodactylus scaber

Description Only recently introduced to this state, adults collected in Texas measure up to about 4½ inches from snout to tip of tail, with original tail. Most collected specimens, however, have regenerated tails that are much shorter than an original. An original tail makes up more than half the total length. This small gecko is generally beige above and whitish below. The dorsum is covered with brown spots in regular arrangement. It may have a curved brown mark on the back of the neck. The tail has dark brown bands. The head is of moderate size, and the snout is slightly elongated. All 4 feet have long toes. The tail is slightly flattened.

Range First collected in Galveston, near the port, in 1983, this gecko is native to Egypt, south to the Sudan, and west into India. It seems to have established a breeding colony in Galveston in the same area where the introduced Mediterranean gecko is known to thrive.

Habitat In its native lands, its habitat is primarily desert, but the colony established in Galveston is quite at home in human habitations and in and around other buildings.

Behavior Insufficient studies have been done to establish distinct behavioral characteristics beyond that it is nocturnal and seems to be similar in habits to the Mediterranean gecko.

Reproduction The colony in Galveston does appear to be breeding successfully, but distinct reproductive behavior is not yet recorded.

Mediterranean Gecko
Hemidactylus turcicus

Description   4 to 5 inches at maturity, from snout to tip of tail, with slender tail about half of total length. This pale, translucent lizard has small but obvious light and dark spots formed by tubercles on all dorsal body areas. Juveniles have dark banded tails. Its large lidless eyes give it an alert appearance. Toes have broad pads nearly their full length and claws extending beyond the pads.

Range   Native to the Mediterranean area, the Middle East, and India, this gecko was introduced to Texas and has prospered here. It is common throughout the southern part of the state. Apparently isolated populations are found in metropolitan areas in northeastern and Central Texas.

Habitat   It is the gecko most easily seen because it is common in human habitations. It also seeks shelter under palm fronds, in rough-textured tree bark, and in rocky outcroppings. It is often seen on lighted billboards at night and on slanted ceilings of condominiums on South Padre Island.

Behavior   This gecko is nocturnal and will position itself on walls or ceilings of habitations near lights where insects gather. It is territorial and has been observed to fight to defend a good location. Males squeak during fights and at other times, as well, possibly to signal territorial claim.

Reproduction   Breeding takes place for 4 or 5 months beginning in March, and clutches of 1 or 2 eggs are laid beginning in April. During the breeding period, eggs can be seen through the translucent skin on the abdomen of the female.

Green Anole

Anolis carolinensis

Note Commonly called a chameleon, this lizard is not a true chameleon.

Description 5 to 8 inches from snout to tip of slender, round tail, which can be twice as long as head and body length. Females tend to be smaller than males. Color varies from intense green to dark brown and through every combination of those colors while changing. In all color variations, this lizard is generally paler on the ventral side of its head and on its throat. Some specimens have a narrow, mottled dark brown or white stripe down the spine. Males have a prominent dewlap that when extended displays a bright pink. Females may show faint indications of pink on the throat. Claws extend beyond the toe pads on each foot of both sexes.

Range Common throughout the eastern half of Texas except for desert areas along the lower coast. A separate population is found in the Lower Rio Grande Valley.

Habitat This arboreal lizard climbs high in trees but can also be found on shrubs, vines, and ground cover, as well as on fences and the walls of buildings. It requires the shelter of shade and a moist environment.

Behavior It is diurnal but can often be seen sleeping on twigs at night because the skin reflects the beam of a flashlight. Color change can be sudden and is stimulated by a number of factors, including temperature, emotion, and light quality. Males are combative, using the throat fan for confrontations. They may chase one another at great speed high into trees and may fall from heights without harm. This lizard eats insects and small spiders and sometimes appears to stalk prey in slow motion. It sheds its skin several times a year and usually consumes the shed, peeling it away with its mouth.

Reproduction Breeding occurs over 7 months, beginning in March or April. Single white soft-shelled eggs are laid in loose leaf litter or other moist debris. Hatchlings of 2$\frac{1}{16}$ to 2$\frac{5}{8}$ inches emerge after 5 to 7 weeks.

Brown Anole
Anolis sagrei

Description   5 to 8 inches from snout to tip of slender, compressed tail, which can be twice as long as head and body length. Females tend to be smaller than males. General coloration is light brown, with a narrow, light middorsal stripe. On either side of the light stripe there may be dark semicircles down the back. The pattern usually fades with age. When the dewlap, or throat fan, is not extended, males show a light streak on the throat and chest. When extended, the dewlap is red-orange with a white or yellowish center stripe. It may have several rows of light spots. The snout is shorter than that of the green anole. As on the green anole, the claws of this lizard extend beyond the well-developed toe pads.

Range   Native to Cuba, this lizard has been introduced to Texas by way of Florida, possibly carried here in the pots of houseplants. It is known to be in the Houston area.

Habitat   This lizard thrives in an environment with plenty of rain. It is usually seen on trees, shrubs, or fences and walls not more than 6 feet above the ground.

Behavior   This diurnal lizard is primarily terrestrial, even though it can climb with ease. When it is at rest on a surface above the ground, it positions itself with the head down. On the ground, it may hop to evade capture. Unlike the green anole, it does not change color. Males are territorial and ward off intruders by elaborately bobbing the head while displaying the dewlap. It eats a variety of insects and small spiders and makes quick dashes to catch its prey. It sheds its skin several times a year.

Reproduction   Breeding takes place throughout the spring and summer. The female lays a single egg about every 2 weeks from spring through September. Incubation lasts about 30 days.

Southwestern Earless Lizard

Cophosaurus texanus scitulus

Description   2⅝ to 7¼ inches from snout to tip of tail, with tail length about the same as head-body length. Females are considerably smaller than males. This brilliantly colored lizard has a grayish ground color, and male markings are more colorful than the female's. The male may show orange, green, yellow, and even pink, as well as the characteristic pairs of curved black lines in a field of blue just in front of the hind legs. The black lines wrap around onto the belly, where they end on either side of the midventral line. Both sexes have distinct black bars on the ventral surface of the tail, and these may be evident across the dorsal surface, where small dark flecks begin to fuse into bands. It has no external ear openings, and the body and tail appear slightly flattened. The hind legs are distinctly longer than the forelegs, and the toes are quite long. The female may have a dark stripe on the back side of each thigh, set off by surrounding lighter pigment. The thigh stripe may be evident in juveniles, as well, but not as distinct in males.

Range   Found only in far West Texas, west of the Pecos, in the Big Bend and adjacent areas. It is common in its range.

Habitat   A rock-dwelling lizard, it prefers dry rocky streambeds or broken rock around limestone cliffs.

Behavior   A diurnal lizard, it is speedy and can be seen dashing from rock to rock, rarely stopping on flat open ground. As it runs, it curves its long banded tail over its back. It may wave the tail from side to side in the upraised position when coming to a halt or when about to dash off again. It feeds on a variety of insects, including beetles, grasshoppers, and larvae.

Reproduction   During breeding the coloration of the male intensifies, and when gravid, the female may have quite pink flanks. Eggs are laid from March to August, and hatchlings measure about 2 inches.

Texas Earless Lizard

Cophosaurus texanus texanus

Description   2¾ to 7⅛ inches from snout to tip of tail, with tail slightly longer than head and body. Females are smaller than males. This lizard varies in coloration depending on habitat and may be brownish, grayish, or reddish, with lighter flecks covering the dorsal surface. It has no external ear openings, and both body and tail appear slightly flattened. The hind legs are distinctly longer than the forelegs, and the toes are quite long. It has 2 folds on its throat and relatively large eyes. Both sexes have distinct black bars on the ventral surface of the long tail, and these are somewhat evident across the dorsal surface as well, where small dark markings begin to fuse into bands. Additionally, the male has 2 prominent black curving marks on each side just in front of the hind legs and wrapping around onto the belly, where they widen and stop abruptly on either side of the midventral line. The pairs of curved black lines are surrounded by blue. The female lacks both the curved lines and the blue coloration.

Range   Found throughout north-central and west-central Texas and along the Rio Grande, but not including the Big Bend or the Lower Rio Grande Valley.

Habitat   This terrestrial lizard inhabits rocky areas, such as dry streambeds and open rocky desert flats. It can also be found in areas with limestone cliffs and broken rocks, which it can use for shelter.

Behavior   A diurnal lizard, it is speedy and can be seen dashing from rock to rock, rarely stopping on flat open ground. As it runs, it curves its long banded tail over its back. It may wave the tail from side to side in the upraised position when coming to a halt or when about to dash off again. When it is threatened, it may run a short distance, then stop abruptly on a rock on which it seems to disappear, such is the extent of its protective coloration. It feeds on a variety of insects, including beetles, grasshoppers, and larvae.

Reproduction It lays eggs from March to August, and hatch-lings measure about 2 inches. When gravid, females are more brilliantly colored, with orange on the throat and pink on both sides.

Eastern Collared Lizard

Crotaphytus collaris collaris

Description   8 to 14 inches from snout to tip of long tail. This colorful lizard is easily recognized by 2 distinct black collar markings on its slender neck and by its large head. Its body is rounded and the tail quite slender and possibly patterned by small brown spots forming bars. The ground color and pattern vary widely depending on location, age, and sex of specimen, as well as other factors. Generally, markings fade with age, except for collars. The dorsal ground color varies from emerald-green to blue to grayish brown and pale yellow. All dorsal surfaces, including face, limbs, and tail, are dotted with white spots, and darker yellowish or reddish bands may cross the body. The female tends to be less vivid in color but has bright orange spots on her sides and neck when carrying eggs. Both sexes are more colorful during the breeding season. Other characteristics include small granular scales and a large mouth that is dark inside.

Range   Found throughout the western and central regions of Texas and north through the Panhandle.

Habitat   It is a rock-dwelling lizard, but since it is not a good climber, it is most commonly seen on rock piles, basking on gentle slopes, in gullies, or on limestone ledges. It is most abundant in hilly areas where rocks provide convenient cover and where there is open space for running.

Behavior   This diurnal lizard has 2 outstanding behavioral characteristics: it is a voracious feeder, eating just about anything smaller than itself, including insects, spiders, lizards, and snakes; and when it runs at top speed, which it often does chasing prey or in retreat, it lifts its forelegs and body off the ground and speeds along bipedally, with forelegs close to its body. It may even lift its long tail to decrease drag. It is a wary and elusive lizard, but when retreat is not possible, it will stand its ground with mouth open. If captured it will attempt to bite. This lizard is also an agile jumper and readily leaps from one rock to another. When alarmed it swiftly takes cover in rock crevices or burrows.

Reproduction Egg clutches are laid in midsummer in loose sand or tunnels under rocks. The hatchlings are dramatically marked with broad dark bands across the body and tail. Yellowish bands may alternate with those, and red bars may be present for a short time after hatching.

Chihuahuan Collared Lizard

Crotaphytus collaris fuscus

Description   8 to 14 inches from snout to tip of long, rounded tail. This lizard has 2 distinct black collar markings on its slender neck. Its head is broad, and the mouth is large and dark inside. The dorsal surfaces are yellowish brown to brown with small light spots. It may have dark brown bands across the body. The scales on the body are small and smooth; those on the tail are a little larger. During breeding season, the female usually has red-orange spots, sometimes forming bars, on both sides.

Range   Found in the extreme western tip of the state.

Habitat   A rock-dwelling lizard, it is most commonly seen on rock piles, basking on slopes, in gullies, or especially on limestone ledges with crevices. It tolerates an arid climate.

Behavior   Like the eastern collared lizard, this one has 2 outstanding behavioral characteristics: it is a voracious feeder, eating just about anything smaller than itself, including insects, spiders, lizards, and snakes; and when it runs at top speed, which it often does chasing prey or in retreat, it lifts its front legs and body off the ground and speeds along bipedally, with the front legs close to its body. It may even lift its long tail to decrease drag. It is a wary and elusive lizard, but when retreat is not possible, it will stand its ground with mouth open. If captured, it will attempt to bite. It is an agile jumper and readily leaps from one rock to another. When alarmed it swiftly takes cover in rock crevices.

Reproduction   Breeding takes place from April to June, and the female deposits up to 12 eggs in sandy soil or burrows during midsummer. The head-body length of hatchlings is about 3½ inches, and they are marked with light and dark crossbars.

Reticulate Collared Lizard

Crotaphytus reticulatus

Description   8 to 16¾ inches from snout to tip of tail. This large, fat-bodied lizard has a large head and slender neck. Its slightly flattened tail is a little more than twice the length of the head and body. All 4 limbs are strong, and the hind legs are nearly twice as long as the forelegs. The ground color on dorsal surfaces is gray to warm brown. Ventral surfaces are an unmarked cream color or yellowish cream. The back, tail, and limbs are patterned with light-colored lines that form a network, and there are large black spots arranged inside the network in rows on the back. Males and females are similar, but colors can vary greatly during breeding periods. During the breeding season, males may have black collar markings and a bright yellow chest and forelegs. Females may have pink throats and when gravid display red bars on their sides.

Range   Found in South Texas on the Rio Grande plains, but not including the coastal areas.

Habitat   Inhabits brushlands along the river, also escarpments, banks of arroyos, and convenient rockpiles or packrat burrows.

Behavior   This active lizard is diurnal and quick to take cover when threatened in the least. If retreat is impossible, it will make itself imposing by arching its back and displaying its open mouth. It feeds readily on many kinds of insects, spiders, smaller lizards and snakes, and small mammals.

Reproduction   Females lay 8 to 11 eggs in midsummer, which hatch in 60 to 90 days. Hatchlings are 3½ to 4 inches long and are light gray with yellow or yellow-orange crossbands and rows of black spots.

Broad-ringed Spiny-tailed Iguana

Ctenosaura pectinata

Description At maturity this enormous lizard may be 48 inches long, with the tail about twice as long as the head and body. The body is stout, and the head is broad with a tapering snout. The legs are strong, and the hind legs are considerably larger than the front legs. The toes are quite long and have long, sharp claws. General coloration is gray to yellowish brown, and it has vague, broad dark crossbars. The legs are darker than the body and tail. The scales on the body are small and smooth, except for a prominent crest of keeled scales down the middle of the back, more noticeable on the male. On the tail keeled scales form prominent rings every second or third scale row.

Range Native to Mexico, this lizard is now seen occasionally in the extreme southern tip of the state, near Brownsville.

Habitat It is at home in a rocky terrain where crevices and holes provide hiding places.

Behavior This lizard is diurnal and extremely wary, taking refuge in a crevice or under a rock at the least sign of approach. It may climb onto the trunk of a nearby tree if threatened. It bobs its head to signal a territorial claim or during breeding. It eats vegetation including flowers, fruits, leaves, and small stems.

Reproduction Breeding takes place in early spring, and the female lays a clutch of up to 50 eggs in burrows during April or May.

Longnose Leopard Lizard

Gambelia wislizenii wislizenii

Description 8½ to 15⅛ inches from snout to tip of tail. This lizard is large and slender at maturity. Its tail may be twice as long as the head-body length, and it is round rather than flattened. Color and pattern may vary depending on temperature, soil of habitat, activity, and other factors. Generally, the ground color is light gray or brown with dark spots on the body and tail. The spots may vary from brown to nearly black. Ventral surfaces are pale, and in dark phases this lizard may have light transverse lines on the sides of the body that extend upward onto the dorsal surface. The narrow, elongated head may or may not be spotted, but limbs and tail are usually marked the same as the body, making the lizard difficult to see on sandy soil.

Range Found in far West Texas, from El Paso through the Trans-Pecos region and Big Bend.

Habitat An inhabitant of flat, arid or semiarid desert areas with little vegetation and loose, sandy soil; seems to prefer widely spaced clumps of vegetation where it may take shelter or wait for prey.

Behavior This diurnal lizard is speedy, dashing from one clump of vegetation to another, and may flatten itself to avoid detection. It feeds on large insects, spiders, and smaller lizards, even its own species. It may leap to catch flying insects. It is an alert and active lizard and may hiss when threatened. It will almost certainly bite if captured.

Reproduction Females usually exhibit special coloration just before depositing eggs. Reddish orange bars or spots appear on the sides, sometimes on the ventral side of the tail, and sometimes on the flanks. Up to 7 eggs are laid in early summer, and a second clutch may be laid in August. Hatchlings are about 5 inches long and may have reddish spots.

Plateau Earless Lizard

Holbrookia lacerata lacerata

Description 4½ to 6 inches from snout to tip of tail, with tail making up about half of total length. This small, slightly flattened lizard has no external ears and is usually gray, with distinct dark spots in 3 locations. Dorsally, spots appear in pairs along its entire length, with pale rims around each spot. The underside of the tail is also marked with round, dark spots, and there may be separate elongated spots or bars along its sides between the legs. Male, female, and immature are all similar in color and pattern, except for gravid females. Just before a female deposits eggs, her neck and back may turn light green.

Range This subspecies is found only in the Edwards Plateau region of Central Texas.

Habitat It inhabits sandy, generally dry upland areas with brush and sparse low-growing vegetation.

Behavior This diurnal lizard is wary and will dash off at high speed, sometimes disappearing into sand to avoid being caught.

Reproduction It lays clutches of eggs in spring and perhaps again in late summer. Incubation requires 4 to 5 weeks, and hatchlings are about 1½ inches long, including tail.

Southern Earless Lizard

Holbrookia lacerata subcaudalis

Description   4½ to 6 inches from snout to tip of tail. This earless lizard has 2 rows of dark spots down each side of its grayish back. It has distinct round dark spots on the underside of its tail and may have several dark bars along its sides. All ages and sexes are similarly marked, except for breeding females, which may have light green necks and backs.

Range   This lizard is found only in South Texas below the Balcones Escarpment, along the Rio Grande, and east almost to the Gulf of Mexico, but not including the Lower Rio Grande Valley.

Habitat   Like the plateau earless lizard, this lizard inhabits generally dry, sandy areas with sparse vegetation.

Behavior   This lizard is diurnal and seeks shelter under loose sand if threatened.

Reproduction   It lays eggs in late spring and perhaps again in late summer. Hatchlings emerge after 4 to 5 weeks and are about 1½ inches long.

Speckled Earless Lizard

Holbrookia maculata approximans

Description   4 to 5 inches including tail, with tail accounting for about half that length. This lizard has no external ear openings and no markings on the underside of the tail, and longitudinal stripes on the dorsum are indistinct except on the neck. The dorsal surface has obscure blotches on a grayish brown ground color, with obvious white specks overall. Both sexes have pairs of black diagonal marks on the sides, just behind the forelegs. On the male those marks are rimmed in blue. They are less distinct on females. During breeding the female will show rich orange coloration on the throat and sides, sometimes on the back, and behind the rear legs.

Range   This subspecies occurs along the Pecos River and in the extreme western tip of the state.

Habitat   This lizard is found in sandy desert grasslands and along the dry edges of the riverbed, as well as in open sandy basins.

Behavior   This diurnal lizard is particularly active in the morning, foraging in the open for insects and small spiders. It may seek shelter in burrows or partially bury itself in sand.

Reproduction   Breeding occurs in spring and summer. Hatchlings are 1½ inches long.

Northern Earless Lizard

Holbrookia maculata maculata

Description 4 to 5 inches from snout to tip of tail, with tail making up half or less of total length. This small lizard has no external ear openings and no markings on the underside of the tail. It is usually grayish brown and is often difficult to distinguish from its surroundings. The dorsal pattern is made up of rows of medium to dark blotches with pale rims. There are also lengthwise stripes, paler than the ground color, on the back from eye to hind leg and along the side from leg to leg. It has a pale middorsal line and overall covering of small white dots. Both sexes have pairs of black diagonal marks on the sides, just behind the forelegs. On the male, those marks may be rimmed in blue. On the female, they are less distinct and lack the blue. However, during breeding season the female usually exhibits rich orange coloration along lengthwise stripes, as well as on the sides and throat.

Range This subspecies is found throughout the Panhandle above a roughly diagonal line from Hardeman County southwest to Winkler County.

Habitat A ground-dwelling lizard, it can be found in a number of habitats that have sandy soil or fine gravel, including open prairies, sandy grasslands, dry streambeds, or farm fields.

Behavior This small diurnal lizard is not especially shy and may remain motionless, partially buried in sand, when approached. When threatened it will retreat to nearby burrows or dive into loose sand. It feeds on insects and small spiders.

Reproduction Breeding occurs in spring and early summer. Hatchlings are about 1½ inches long and have a pattern similar to the breeding color of females.

Eastern Earless Lizard

Holbrookia maculata perspicua

Description   4 to 5 inches from snout to tip of tail, with tail making up half or less of total length. This lizard has no external ear openings and no markings on the underside of the tail. It is usually grayish brown and similar to the color of surrounding soil. The dorsal pattern is made up of rows of distinct medium to dark blotches on both sides of the middorsal line. It has a pale middorsal stripe from the head onto the tail, and it may have other lengthwise stripes paler than the ground color. The male has a pair of dark diagonal marks on each side near the foreleg, and they may be surrounded by blue. The female may have only a suggestion of those marks on the side, but she will have a cover of white flecks that the male usually lacks.

Range   This subspecies is found in the central portion of northern Texas.

Habitat   This ground-dwelling lizard can be found in a number of habitats with sandy or loamy soil, most often on prairies.

Behavior   This lizard is active during the day, particularly in the morning, and it feeds on insects and small spiders. It may seek shelter in small mammal burrows or partially bury itself in the sand.

Reproduction   Breeding occurs in spring and early summer. Hatchlings are about 1½ inches long.

Keeled Earless Lizard

Holbrookia propinqua propinqua

Description   4½ to 5½ inches from snout to tip of tail, with tail as long as or longer than the head-body length and with notably long hind legs. This small lizard has tiny keeled scales on its back and no external ear. Its overall color is greenish gray to brown, and though the female is generally paler than the male, both have pale unmarked ventral surfaces on body and tail. Dorsal pattern varies, but males have 2 dark diagonal lines on each side just behind the foreleg. The dorsum is covered with white specks, and there may be dark spots from the shoulder onto the tail, or pale lengthwise stripes running from the head onto the tail, or both. Dark markings are usually rimmed posteriorly with light spots.

Range   Abundant on Padre Island and found throughout much of southern Texas.

Habitat   This lizard lives in loose, shifting sand, especially at the edges of sand dunes on barrier beaches.

Behavior   A diurnal lizard, it can easily be spotted foraging for insects in the sparse vegetation around sand dunes. It can quickly disappear into loose sand to escape capture.

Reproduction   Hatchlings appear in midsummer and are usually 1½ inches long, with well-defined paired dark spots on the dorsum.

Texas Horned Lizard

Phrynosoma cornutum

Description 2½ to 4¼ inches from snout to tip of tail at maturity. Some may be larger; the record is 7⅛ inches. Commonly called the horny toad, this lizard has a broad, flat body, short tail, and short pointed snout. The prominent crown of spines at the back of the head, with 2 enlarged spines in the center, gives the appearance of horns. A row of enlarged spines projects from each side of the throat, and 2 rows of spiny scales rim each side of the body. Belly scales are keeled or ridged lengthwise. Color varies relative to soil of habitat, ranging from a ground color of light brown to tan or gray, with light yellow or reddish tones and white. Distinct markings include dark brown spots with posterior rims of yellow or white just behind the head, on both sides of the middorsal line, and on the back and tail. Spots surround enlarged spines. A narrow streak of pale beige or white extends middorsally from the head onto the base of the tail. Wide dark lines extend downward from the eyes and across the top of the head.

Range Found at all elevations throughout Texas, except for the eastern region, where a separate population is found only in a small area contiguous to Louisiana. Once seen in abundance throughout Texas, this lizard's population was dramatically reduced during the fifties and sixties. It is generally accepted that the reduction in numbers was related to the widespread use of insecticides to eradicate ants, the lizard's main food, and to habitat alteration. These lizards are still abundant west of a line drawn roughly from Abilene to Del Rio.

Habitat Inhabits flat, open, generally dry country with little plant cover, except for bunchgrass and cactus. Strictly terrestrial, this lizard can bury itself in loose soil that is sandy, loamy, or rocky.

Behavior This diurnal lizard is a fast runner, and it seeks shelter under rocks, among low-growing vegetation, or in burrows of other animals. Usually seen only on warm or hot days, it would normally be observed near an ant trail or on an ant mound. It feeds almost exclusively on large live ants. In stress situations, it squirts blood from its eyes. This alarming trait may be seen when the lizard is caught, but it may also occur in conjunction with the shedding of skin. This lizard is seen only during late spring and summer. Hibernation begins in September or October, when weather turns cool, and it continues until late April or May.

Reproduction Mating occurs soon after emergence from hibernation. Females dig burrows 5 to 7 inches deep and lay up to 37 eggs. Incubation lasts 5½ to 7 weeks, depending on ground temperatures, and hatchlings are 1¼ inches from snout to tip of tail.

Mountain Short-horned Lizard

Phrynosoma douglassii hernandesi

Description 2½ to 5⅞ inches from snout to tip of tail. This flat-bodied lizard has short, broad-based, reddish horns that create 2 distinct formations on either side of the back of the head. Its tail is relatively short, and the body is round. It differs from other horned lizards in the same range by having a single row of enlarged light-colored scales fringing its sides. Adults are more colorful than other species. Ground color varies from yellow-beige to light brown or gray, or reddish brown. The underside is smooth, and the chest may be pale orange. The head is usually reddish, and pairs of large dark patches on the neck and back are usually rimmed in the rear in pale yellow.

Range This lizard is known from only 2 small, isolated populations in far West Texas, one in the Guadalupe Mountains and one in the Davis Mountains.

Habitat This lizard is more cold-tolerant than other species of horned lizards, and it inhabits forested areas and semiarid plains at high elevations. Soil type is usually sandy or pebbly, with some loose soil present.

Behavior This lizard is most active at midday and may bury itself in loose soil at night. It hibernates from the first cool weather until midspring. A feisty lizard, it may hiss if threatened, lower its head to project its horns upward, puff up its body to appear menacing, and squirt blood from its eyes. It feeds mainly on ants and sometimes on beetles and snails.

Reproduction This species is live-bearing. It mates in spring, soon after it emerges from hibernation, and the young are born in July and August. The young are 1 to 1½ inches at birth, and there may be as many as 30 in a litter.

Roundtail Horned Lizard

Phrynosoma modestum

Description   3 to 4⅛ inches at maturity. This flat-bodied lizard has quite a short tail (about half the head-body length), which is broad at the base and tapers abruptly to a slender rounded shape. It has a crown of 4 short horns that are about equal in length and separated at the base. And it can easily be distinguished from other horned lizards by the absence of a fringe of scales along its sides. It also lacks ear openings. Overall coloration varies depending on immediate habitat, and this lizard so closely matches the texture and color of the soil of its environment as to be almost invisible unless in motion. Variations range from grayish white or yellowish gray to several shades of light brown or reddish brown. It has dark brown patches on each side of the neck and groin. The groin patches may extend forward on the sides. It may also have dark patches on the base of the tail. The undersides are pale gray and usually unmarked.

Range   Found in most of the western part of the state and Panhandle, but not across the top of the Panhandle.

Habitat   Inhabits arid or semiarid desert plains with scrubby vegetation and sandy or gravelly soil. It may also be found in washes with small rocks.

Behavior   This diurnal lizard is well camouflaged and when threatened will remain still, flattening itself against the soil to avoid detection. If it is forced to flee, it will make a short dash and stop abruptly, flattening itself again. This lizard hibernates in the winter, usually burying itself in a burrow. Its primary food is ants, but it may also eat beetles.

Reproduction   It lays egg clutches in early summer, and hatchlings are small, about 1 inch long.

Blue Spiny Lizard

Sceloporus cyanogenys

Description   5 to 14¼ inches from snout to tip of tail, with tail up to 1½ times as long as the head-body length. This is probably the largest of the spiny lizards, and at maturity the male is brilliantly colored and boldly marked. The back and tail are intense metallic blue-green and may have some light flecks. The tail is somewhat banded with dusky and light areas. It has a broad dark band behind the neck, wrapping around the shoulders like a shawl. The dark band is bordered on both sides with white. The head and limbs are dark brown with light flecks, and limbs may have vague dark bands. The male also has a light blue chin and throat and a blue patch on each side of the belly, with dark borders on inner edges. The female is gray or brown and lacks the metallic blue sheen and belly patches. It may have narrow dark crossbands on the back and limbs. The young resemble the female.

Range   This lizard is found in the western portion of South Texas, along the Rio Grande, but not including the lower river valley and mouth.

Habitat   This lizard inhabits rocky cliffs, dry earth stream banks, boulders, and sometimes man-made structures, such as rock walls, bridges, and piles of construction materials.

Behavior   This diurnal lizard prefers a diet of flying insects, but it also eats a variety of other insects. It seeks shelter under or between rocks and in earth crevices.

Reproduction   This lizard bears its young in litters of up to 18 babies. They are born from February into June and are 2½ to 2¾ inches long at birth.

Dunes Sagebrush Lizard

Sceloporus graciosus arenicolous

Description   4½ to 6¼ inches from snout to tip of tail, with tail usually just slightly longer than the head-body length. This pale light brown lizard has only faint dorsal markings that may include a gray stripe running from its head onto its tail. The male has blue patches on its belly that are bordered midventrally with black but which fade outward. Neither sex has any blue on the throat, but both usually have a small dark patch in front of each foreleg. The female may have pinkish coloration on sides and neck. Both sexes have small granular scales on the rear of the thigh.

Range   In Texas this lizard is found only in the sand dunes near Monahans.

Habitat   Found only on or very near active sand dunes with low-growing vegetation under which it can take refuge.

Behavior   Its pale coloration camouflages this lizard well on the sand. When alarmed it may dash for a distance over the dune, then stop, nearly invisible. It is diurnal and may take shelter under bushes or bury itself in sand if threatened.

Reproduction   It lays a single clutch of eggs in early summer, which hatches about 4 weeks later.

Mesquite Lizard

Sceloporus grammicus microlepidotus

Description 4 to 6⅞ inches from snout to tip of tail, with the slender tail usually a little longer than the head-body length. This spiny lizard is relatively flat-bodied, and its camouflage is nearly perfect for its usual tree-trunk habitat. The general coloration is medium gray to olive, with a somewhat mottled look. It has 3 to 6 narrow, dark wavy crossbars on the back, which may be more obvious on females. The forelegs and tail may also have distinct narrow crossbars. The male has a dark vertical line on each shoulder, pale blue patches on each side of the belly and on the throat, and black mottling on the throat. The inner edges of the blue belly patches may be bordered in black. Close inspection of the neck scales shows that those on the side of the neck are much smaller than those on top.

Range This lizard is found in extreme South Texas and in an isolated population near Corpus Christi.

Habitat Found in arid and semiarid portions of its range where mesquite and other low-growing trees provide its home. It is usually found on mesquite trees.

Behavior This diurnal lizard is shy, spends most of its time high in trees, and can dart upward out of sight without the slightest noise. It is rarely observed because it usually retreats to the back of a branch or trunk and flees upward before the observer is within sighting distance.

Reproduction It mates in the fall and gives birth from January into early spring. Litter size averages 6, and the newborns are about 1¾ inches total length.

Twin-spotted Spiny Lizard

Sceloporus magister bimaculosus

Description   7 to 13 inches from snout to tip of tail, with tail up to 1½ times the head-body length. This usually light-colored lizard has large, prominently pointed scales. General coloration may vary from yellow to light brown, and it may have pale crossbands, which are more prominent in female and juveniles. It has a black wedge-shaped mark with a pale rear margin on each side of the neck, just in front of the shoulders, and usually it will have a dark line behind the eye. The male of this sturdy-looking lizard has blue patches on its throat and belly. It may have 2 rows of dark spots running down its back, and its limbs may be finely striped. The female does not exhibit the blue markings.

Range   It is found in the Trans-Pecos region of Texas.

Habitat   This lizard can be found on arid or semiarid plains or on lower slopes, below 4,000 feet, where there is sufficient vegetation, rock, or debris to provide cover.

Behavior   This diurnal lizard climbs easily on rocks, walls, and trees when foraging for insects. It may also eat other lizards, as well as some buds or tender leaves. It is quite wary and will seek cover in vegetation, crevices, or mammal burrows when threatened.

Reproduction   Mating takes place in spring and early summer, and hatchlings emerge about 10 weeks after deposition of eggs. Hatchlings are about 3 inches total length.

Big Bend Canyon Lizard

Sceloporus merriami annulatus

Description   4½ to 6¼ inches from snout to tip of tail, with tail usually a little more than 1½ times head-body length. The 3 canyon lizards have small scales, and they are distinguished by an abrupt change in the size of scales from the dorsal surface of the neck to the sides. The scales on the sides of the neck are much smaller than those on top. In general, the side scales are granular, and the dorsal scales are keeled. Male and female are similar on the dorsal surfaces. This spiny lizard is gray to tan to brown, depending on the color of the habitat. The Big Bend canyon lizard has 2 rows of dark spots running down each side of its back and a distinct black vertical line on each shoulder. The limbs and tail may be faintly banded. The male is much more vividly marked on the ventral surface, with blue patches on the sides of the belly and dark lines on the throat. The underside of the tail has dark crossbands. Those markings are absent or faint on the female. Both sexes have external ear openings, a partially developed fold on the throat, and a fairly distinct dewlap, although it is smaller on the female.

Range   This lizard is found only in the higher elevations of the Big Bend region in Brewster County.

Habitat   This rock-dwelling lizard may be found on canyon walls or other rocky slopes, as well as on boulders and rocky outcrops where there is little or no vegetation.

Behavior   This lizard is diurnal and not particularly shy. It may seek shelter in a crevice if threatened but usually will reappear quickly.

Reproduction   It lays eggs from spring through early summer, and hatchlings are about 2 inches long.

Presidio Canyon Lizard

Sceloporus merriami longipunctatus

Description   4½ to 6¼ inches from snout to tip of tail, with tail usually a little more than 1½ times head-body length. The 3 canyon lizards have small scales, and they are distinguished by an abrupt change in the size of scales from the dorsal surface of the neck to the sides. The scales on the sides of the neck are much smaller than those on top. In general, the side scales are granular, and the dorsal scales are keeled. Male and female are similar on the dorsal surfaces. This spiny lizard is gray to tan to brown, depending on the color of the habitat. The Presidio canyon lizard has 2 rows of dark, curved marks down its back and a distinct black vertical line on each shoulder. The limbs and tail may be banded. The male may have blue patches on the sides of the belly, and both sexes have dark lines on the throat and dark bars on the underside of the tail. Both sexes have external ear openings, a partially developed fold on the throat, and a fairly distinct dewlap, although it is smaller in the female.

Range   This lizard is found only in Presidio County.

Habitat   This rock-dwelling lizard may be found on canyon walls or other rocky slopes, as well as on boulders and rocky outcrops where there is little or no vegetation.

Behavior   This lizard is diurnal and not particularly shy. It may seek shelter in a crevice if threatened but usually will reappear quickly.

Reproduction   It lays eggs from spring through early summer, and hatchlings are about 2 inches long.

Merriam's Canyon Lizard

Sceloporus merriami merriami

Description   4½ to 6¼ inches from snout to tip of tail, with tail usually a little more than 1½ times head-body length. The palest and least marked of the 3 canyon lizards, this one is gray or light brown, perhaps with a blue cast. It has a row of dark spots on either side of the middorsal line, a row of faint spots down each side, and a prominent dark vertical mark on each side of the neck. Its body is covered with small, pale spots, but the ventral surfaces are only faintly marked, if at all. It has a partially developed fold on its throat and a fairly distinct dewlap, even in the female. It has external ear openings and small scales overall. A distinguishing feature of the canyon lizards is the abrupt change in size of scales from the dorsal surface of the neck to the sides of the neck. The scales on the sides are much smaller than those on top.

Range   Found in the western part of the Edwards Plateau, from the eastern edge of Brewster County to Edwards County.

Habitat   This rock-dwelling lizard may be found on canyon walls or other rocky slopes where there is little or no vegetation.

Behavior   This lizard is diurnal and not particularly shy. It may seek shelter in a crevice if threatened but usually will reappear quickly.

Reproduction   It lays eggs from spring through early summer, and hatchlings are about 2 inches long.

Texas Spiny Lizard

Sceloporus olivaceus

Description 7½ to 11 inches from snout to tip of tail, with tail up to 1¾ times as long as the head-body length. This large, extremely spiny lizard is generally rusty brown and closely resembles the tree bark on which it lives. Its markings vary widely from one individual to another. Most males have a small blue patch on each side of the belly and sometimes light dorsolateral stripes. The female has dark wavy lines across the back and sometimes on the legs close to the body. It has long toes to accommodate climbing.

Range Found throughout north-central, Central, and South Texas.

Habitat This arboreal lizard may be seen in a variety of trees in its range, but it seems to favor mesquite. It may also be seen on structures such as fences, barns, old houses, bridges, and telephone poles. It is common in wooded urban areas.

Behavior This diurnal lizard is a skillful climber and will flee upward if threatened. It is so inconspicuous when at rest on a tree trunk that it is easily overlooked, but when approached it usually rushes up the trunk, calling attention to itself by the scratchy clamor as it runs.

Reproduction Mating begins in early spring, and egg-laying continues throughout the summer. A female may deposit up to 4 clutches in a year, and a mature individual may lay up to 25 eggs in a clutch. The young are about 2½ inches at hatching.

Crevice Spiny Lizard

Sceloporus poinsettii poinsettii

Description   5 to 11½ inches from snout to tip of tail, with tail up to 1⅔ times as long as the head-body length. This large, rough-scaled lizard may vary in color from yellow to olive and may even appear reddish. The most conspicuous markings are a broad black collar, rimmed front and back by light-colored scales, and a distinctly dark-banded tail. At birth, both sexes are boldly marked with crossbands from snout to tip of tail and may have a narrow dark line down the length of the spine. The female usually retains the early markings, but the male retains only the neck and tail crossbands. The male develops bright blue patches on the throat and on each side of the belly, and those are banded with black on the inner edges.

Range   Found in the Edwards Plateau of Central Texas and throughout the Trans-Pecos region.

Habitat   This rock-dwelling lizard is found in arid and semiarid parts of its range, in rocky canyons, on limestone and other rocky outcrops, and on boulders.

Behavior   A diurnal lizard, it eats insects and sometimes flower buds and tender leaves. It is quick and elusive, moving to the opposite side of the rock when approached and darting into a crevice when threatened directly.

Reproduction   This lizard gives birth to up to 11 young during June and July. The babies are 2½ to 3 inches long at birth.

Southern Prairie Lizard

Sceloporus undulatus consobrinus

Description   3½ to 7 inches from snout to tip of tail, with tail up to 1½ times as long as the head and body. The female may be slightly larger than the male at maturity. The general coloration is light warm brown, and the dorsal surface is marked with a light stripe beginning on each side of the neck and running back onto the base of the tail. There may be dark spots along the light stripes, as well as dark bands across the wide middorsal band of gray or light brown from the nape of the neck onto the tail. The ventral surface of the male has 2 light blue patches along each side of the belly, each one black-bordered and separated from the other. There may be 2 black-bordered blue patches on the throat as well. The female lacks markings on the ventral surfaces, except for perhaps a small blue area on the throat.

Range   Found throughout the western half of Texas, not including the extreme northeastern corner of the Panhandle or the extreme southern tip of the state.

Habitat   This lizard may be seen in a wide variety of habitats, from sand dunes to rocky hillsides. It seems to prefer rocky areas, where rocks provide shelter and basking surfaces.

Behavior   This diurnal lizard is terrestrial in more-open prairie habitats and arboreal in the woodlands of its range. It forages for a wide variety of insects. It seems to prefer beetles, but it eats spiders, centipedes, and snails, too. It will dash for cover if approached while foraging.

Reproduction   Breeding takes place from spring throughout summer, and older females may produce several egg clutches in a year. Hatchlings are about 1¾ inches long, and they appear from June to September.

Northern Prairie Lizard

Sceloporus undulatus garmani

Description   3½ to 7 inches from snout to tip of tail, with tail about 1½ times as long as the head and body. The general coloration is light brown, and the dorsal surface is marked with a light stripe beginning on each side of the head and running back onto the base of the tail. There is a wide middorsal band of gray from the head onto the tail. The ventral surface of the male has 2 black-bordered blue patches, one on each side of the belly. Blue throat patches may be present. The female lacks markings on the ventral surfaces.

Range   This lizard is found in the extreme northeastern corner of the Panhandle.

Habitat   It is at home in sandy areas with brush and mammal burrows for shelter.

Behavior   This diurnal lizard is primarily terrestrial and feeds on a variety of insects, preferring beetles. If threatened, it will seek refuge under low brush or in mammal burrows.

Reproduction   Breeding takes place from spring throughout summer, and older females may produce several egg clutches in a year. Hatchlings are about 1¾ inches long.

Northern Fence Lizard

Sceloporus undulatus hyacinthinus

Description   4 to 7½ inches from snout to tip of tail, with tail usually just slightly longer than head-body length. This grayish to brownish lizard is most notable for its blue throat and the 2 bright blue belly patches bordered with black. The blue is most prominent in the male but may be present in the female. This lizard is distinctly marked on the dorsum. Both sexes have a pale dorsolateral stripe extending from the neck onto the tail and another pale stripe along each side of the belly between the front and back legs. Males have a wide dark streak between the pale stripes, from just over the shoulder, down each side, and onto the tail. Both sexes have a dark line along the rear of each thigh, and females may be tinged with orange at the base of the tail. Across the back are a series of broken, dark zigzag marks, more distinct on females.

Range   Found throughout the eastern half of the state, not including the Lower Rio Grande Valley.

Habitat   This lizard is found in a variety of habitats but is most often seen on rail fences, fallen logs, and stumps.

Behavior   This diurnal lizard is primarily a climber and will flee up the nearest tree if encountered on the ground, where it might be foraging for insects. Once on a tree trunk, it will remain on the opposite side from its pursuer, moving up short distances, then stopping. It probably hibernates for 4 months or so during the coldest weather.

Reproduction   Breeding takes place immediately after the lizards emerge from hibernation. Hatchlings are 1⅝ to 2½ inches long and patterned like the female.

Rosebelly Lizard

Sceloporus variabilis marmoratus

Description 3¾ to 5½ inches from snout to tip of tail, with tail about 1⅓ times as long as the head-body length. This subtly marked lizard is generally brown, with the male lighter and the female greener and darker. The 2 most distinct characteristics are not visible as field marks but are unique to this species. The first is a small pocket of skin just behind the rear leg on each side of the tail base. The other is the pink belly coloration found only on the male. The pink patches on each side of the belly are bordered in a dark blue that extends back to the groin and anteriorly upward onto the sides, where it forms a prominent dark spot just behind each foreleg. More obvious as field marks are the light dorsolateral lines that extend from the corner of each eye to the tip of the tail. This lizard also has a row of brown spots down each side of the middorsal line. The spots have light rims behind that may connect to the light dorsolateral lines. The limbs may have dark and light crossbars, some more distinct than others.

Range Found from south-central Texas to the southern tip of the state.

Habitat This lizard inhabits arid regions with cactus, scrubby trees, and brush. It is less often found among rocks.

Behavior Primarily terrestrial, this lizard is also a climber and can be seen on cactus or scrubby trees or even on fence posts. It is diurnal and quite wary but can occasionally be observed on the ground foraging in leaf litter for its favorite food of large insects, such as beetles and even grasshoppers.

Reproduction Mating and egg-laying may occur year-round. The female usually lays eggs in loose earth and dry humus near the base of a small tree.

Eastern Tree Lizard

Urosaurus ornatus ornatus

Description 4 to 6¼ inches from snout to tip of long, slender tail. This lizard is usually gray or grayish brown, depending on its habitat, and its color and pattern provide effective camouflage. The dorsal pattern is made up of irregular dark blotches or crossbands, and some may be edged in a pale blue. Both sexes usually have yellow or pale orange throats. The male usually has a blue belly and blue scales on the orange throat. The legs may be banded. The most significant characteristic distinguishing this from similar species is the variable nature of the dorsal scales. The middorsal scales are small, and on either side are 2 bands of much larger scales, with the bands closest to middorsum being about twice as large as the outer bands. Also quite obvious are the single fold at the throat and folds along the sides of the body that give a wrinkled appearance.

Range This lizard is found in Central Texas and along the Rio Grande River in a narrow band, but not extending into the lower valley.

Habitat A mostly arboreal lizard, it is often seen on fallen trees or nearby rocks. It may also be observed on fence posts or buildings and often is located near streams.

Behavior A diurnal creature, this lizard is quick and skillful at keeping a tree trunk, limb, or rock between itself and any pursuer. Because of that ability and its natural camouflage, it is difficult to observe. It is also likely to dash upward when out of sight. When it is seen, it is likely to be in a vertical position with its head up, and it may make itself slightly more obvious by bobbing its head. It is usually most active in morning and late afternoon, when it forages for its diet of insects and spiders.

Reproduction Egg clutches are large and are laid in spring and throughout summer. Hatchlings are about 1½ inches long and appear from July into October.

Big Bend Tree Lizard

Urosaurus ornatus schmidti

Description   4 to 6¼ inches from snout to tip of long, slender tail. This lizard is usually gray or grayish brown, depending on its habitat, and its color and pattern provide effective camouflage. The dorsal pattern is made up of irregular dark blotches or crossbands, and some may be edged in a pale blue. Both sexes may have yellow or pale orange on the throat. The male usually exhibits 2 separate blue patches on the belly and 1 on the throat. The most significant characteristic distinguishing this from similar species is the variable nature of the dorsal scales. The middorsal scales are small, and on either side are 2 bands of much larger scales, with the bands closest to middorsum a little less than twice as large as the outer bands. Also quite obvious are the single fold on the throat and folds along the sides of the body that give a wrinkled appearance.

Range   This lizard is restricted to the Trans-Pecos area in Texas.

Habitat   In mountainous areas, this lizard is mostly arboreal, but it may also be found climbing on rocks and boulders in areas with few trees.

Behavior   A diurnal lizard, it is quick and skillful at keeping a tree trunk or rock between itself and any pursuer. Because of that ability and its natural camouflage, it is difficult to observe. It is also likely to dash upward when out of sight. When it is seen, it is likely to be in a vertical position with its head up. It is usually most active in morning and late afternoon, when it forages for its diet of insects and spiders.

Reproduction   Egg clutches are large and are laid in spring and throughout summer. Hatchlings are about 1½ inches long and appear from July into October.

Desert Side-blotched Lizard

Uta stansburiana stejnegeri

Description   4 to 6⅜ inches from snout to tip of tail in adult lizards, with tail usually considerably longer than the head-body length. This small lizard is generally brownish but may appear colorful, with subtle blue specks down its back and yellow-orange on its sides. It has external ear openings and a single fold across the throat. The most distinctive characteristic, the one for which it is named, is a dark blue or black blotch on each side just behind the foreleg. Male and female are clearly different from each other, and young of both sexes are much like the female. The adult male has a dorsal pattern of bluish spots and speckles, rarely stripes, and it may have a distinctly turquoise-blue tail. The female exhibits obvious pale, dark-edged stripes from head to base of tail, rarely showing blue.

Range   Found in the Trans-Pecos region and in the eastern part of the lower Panhandle.

Habitat   It is abundant in arid and semiarid areas with sandy soil and rocks or boulders for climbing. In flat desert areas, it may be found where there are scattered rocks or low vegetation and convenient mammal burrows for protection.

Behavior   This diurnal lizard is ground-dwelling, but it also climbs rocks and boulders, if they are convenient to its rather small home territory. It is active throughout the year on warm days, feeding on a wide variety of insects and spiders. If threatened, it will take shelter in a crevice or burrow, often still within view.

Reproduction   This lizard mates throughout the year in favorable weather, and clutches contain 2 to 6 eggs. Hatchlings measure about 2⅓ inches and resemble the female.

Southern
Coal
Skink

Eumeces anthracinus pluvialis

Description   5 to 7 inches from snout to tip of tail, with tail just about twice the length of the head and body. Like all members of the skink family, this one has a long, cylindrical shape and smooth, glossy scales over bony plates, which make the body and tail appear stiff. The tail breaks easily between any vertebrae and regenerates in time. Dorsal coloration is olive-brown, and the male has a reddish color on the head during breeding. Four light stripes extend from the neck back onto the tail, 2 on each side, with the upper stripe on the third and fourth scale rows from the middle of the back. Between the 2 stripes on each side is a dark band 2 to 4 scale rows wide. Ventral surfaces are pale gray or even bluish and unmarked.

Range   Found in the northeastern corner of the state and south into Angelina County.

Habitat   This terrestrial lizard inhabits damp wooded areas with leaf litter and rocky bluffs near streams and creeks.

Behavior   A diurnal lizard, it forages for insects in the moist leaf litter. When threatened it may slip into water to take refuge under rocks or debris.

Reproduction   It lays eggs in June in clutches of 8 or 9. The female usually remains with the clutch until the eggs hatch. Hatchlings are glossy black and unmarked except for faint suggestions of the 4 light stripes. Their tails are bright blue, and lips and snouts may be reddish.

Five-lined Skink

Eumeces faciatus

Description 5 to 8¹⁄₁₆ inches from snout to tip of tail, with tail usually a little less than twice the length of the head and body. Females may be slightly smaller than males. This dark brown skink has small, well-developed limbs, and its patterning varies widely, depending on sex and age. Hatchlings are 2 to 2½ inches in total length and are glossy black with 5 light stripes and bright blue tails. Markings fade with age, as does the ground color. A mature female is usually olive-brown with visible stripes and a grayish tail. A mature male may show no stripes or only traces on the brown or olive ground color. It may also have reddish coloration on the head, particularly during breeding. This skink is quite similar to the broadhead skink. Examination of scales is necessary to distinguish the species from each other. The five-lined has 26 to 30 scale rows at midbody, usually 4 supralabial scales in front of the supralabial scale that touches the eye, and 2 enlarged postlabial scales.

Range Found throughout the eastern half of the state except for the lower coast and Rio Grande Valley.

Habitat This skink is commonly found around human habitations, particularly in gardens and compost heaps. It requires a humid environment and prefers decaying wood or leaf litter.

Behavior This diurnal skink is terrestrial but may climb onto stumps or lower parts of tree trunks. It eats a variety of insects and their larvae as well as spiders, earthworms, and even crawfish, small mice, and lizards.

Reproduction It mates in spring when it emerges from hibernation. The female excavates a nest, deposits the eggs, and tends them until they hatch. Clutches may have up to 15 eggs, and they hatch from June to August.

Broadhead Skink
Eumeces laticeps

Description 6½ to 12¾ inches from snout to tip of tail, with tail up to 1½ times head-body length. Females are usually a little larger than males. This large brown skink, locally called "scorpion," is similar to the five-lined skink. Examination of scales is necessary to distinguish the species from each other. The broadhead has 30 to 32 scale rows at midbody, usually 5 supralabial scales in front of the supralabial scale that touches the eye, and no enlarged postlabial scales. Pattern and colors vary, but the male usually is uniformly olive-brown with a large reddish head and wide jaws. It may have a bluish tail, and there may be faint evidence of 5 light stripes in younger males. Juveniles have distinct light stripes on a glossy black ground color, and bright blue tails. Females usually retain the light stripes, but they fade with age. Overall, the scales are bony, and on the ventral surface of the tail the middle row of scales is wider than other scales.

Range Found throughout the eastern portion of the state, from the Red River south to the central coastal region.

Habitat This skink prefers moist wooded areas but may also be found in urban settings where there is debris and ample leaf litter for shelter.

Behavior This diurnal skink is arboreal and has well-developed limbs and claws adapted for efficient climbing. It may climb high into trees to feed on insects, or it may forage in hollow logs. It has been observed grasping wasp nests in its jaws to shake out pupae for a meal.

Reproduction Mating occurs in April and May. The female lays clutches of up to 16 eggs in depressions under logs or leaf litter and tends the eggs until they hatch. Hatchlings are 2⅜ to 3⅜ inches long and brilliantly marked, with 5 distinct stripes on the back and bright blue tails. They are usually seen from June into August.

Variable Skink

Eumeces multivirgatus epipleurotus

Description   5 to 7⅝ inches from snout to tip of tail, with tail about 1½ times the head-body length. The limbs are rather short. The pattern of this slender, elongated skink varies widely. The ground color is brownish but fades with age, and there are 2 distinct phases, one with many alternating dark and light stripes and the other plain. The stripes also fade with age and may disperse into zigzags. The tail on both phases is wide at the base and narrows gradually. Males may have orange on the lips and extending back to the ear opening.

Range   Found in isolated pockets in far West Texas and in the lower Panhandle.

Habitat   This skink is found in a variety of habitats, from mountains and plateaus to open grassy plains. It may be seen in wooded areas at high elevations or on desert flatlands. Variable skinks in desert habitats are usually of the plain phase, perhaps providing camouflage.

Behavior   This diurnal skink is alert and active. It burrows under rocks, logs, or other debris and feeds on a variety of insects.

Reproduction   Clutches of up to 5 eggs produce hatchlings about 2½ inches long. Juveniles are dark and glossy and have bright blue tails. The striped phase juveniles have a well-defined light middorsal stripe as well as dorsolateral stripes.

Great Plains Skink

Eumeces obsoletus

Description   6½ to 13¾ inches from snout to tip of tail, with tail about 1½ times the head-body length. The largest of the Texas skinks, it varies in color from light tan to olive-brown or gray, with dark-edged scales that create spotting and may appear to form stripes. It is unique in that the scales on its sides are arranged obliquely to those on its back. Its lower sides and belly are yellowish and unmarked. Its tail and limbs are also covered with the dark-edged scales. Its head may be wide at the temporal region.

Range   Found throughout most of Texas, except for the eastern part of the state.

Habitat   It prefers rocky grasslands with loose soil suitable for burrowing. It requires a moist habitat and in arid regions occurs near sources of water.

Behavior   This diurnal skink is rarely seen in the open, preferring to remain under rocks. It eats insects, spiders, and small lizards.

Reproduction   Mating occurs from April to May, and the female excavates a nest where she deposits up to 21 eggs. She tends the eggs until they hatch, in July or August. Hatchlings are about 2½ inches long, with glossy black dorsal scales and bright blue tails. White and orange spots occur on their heads, particularly on the lips.

Southern Prairie Skink

Eumeces septentrionalis obtusirostris

Description   5 to 8⅛ inches from snout to tip of tail, with tail about 20 percent longer than head-body length. This brown skink has short but well-developed limbs and light dorsolateral lines extending from the neck onto the tail. The 2 light lines on each side are separated by a band of brown darker than the middorsal color. The ventral surfaces are light and unmarked.

Range   Found throughout the eastern half of the state, all the way to the Gulf of Mexico but not including the southeastern corner.

Habitat   This skink requires a usually moist environment with rocks for hiding places and leaf litter or other vegetation.

Behavior   This terrestrial skink is active at dusk and in predawn hours, foraging for its prey of insects, spiders, and snails. It usually remains near vegetation and retreats readily if disturbed. It may seek refuge in a convenient burrow.

Reproduction   Mating occurs in May and June, and clutches may have up to 18 eggs. During breeding the male may show orange on its head. Young have brilliant blue tails.

Short-lined Skink

Eumeces tetragrammus brevilineatus

Description   5 to 7 inches from snout to tip of tail, with tail about twice the head-body length, perhaps slightly less. The long cylindrical body and tail are covered with smooth, glossy scales over bony plates. This skink appears stiff in its movements, and the tail breaks easily between any vertebrae, regenerating in time. Its small limbs are weak. Dorsal coloration may vary from brown to olive-green. Two light stripes extend from above and below each eye backward over the neck onto the shoulder, then fade behind the forelegs. The upper stripe on each side lies along the fourth scale row from the middle of the back. Between the light stripes on each side is a broad dark band. The male may have brilliant orange from its nose backward along both upper and lower lips and onto the sides of its throat. Adults of both sexes have a light Y on top of the head.

Range   Found throughout all of Central Texas, down to the northwestern part of South Texas and west to the Big Bend region.

Habitat   This terrestrial lizard inhabits wooded rocky areas at the bases of hills, usually in leaf litter and rotting logs.

Behavior   A diurnal lizard, it forages in brush and leaf litter for its insect prey. It seeks shelter under rocks or convenient debris, including trash piles.

Reproduction   The female lays clutches of 5 to 12 eggs in shallow depressions and remains with her eggs until they hatch. Hatchlings are about 2 inches long, with prominent light stripes and bright blue tails.

Four-lined Skink

Eumeces tetragrammus tetragrammus

Description 5 to 7⅛ inches from snout to tip of tail, with tail about 1⅔ times the head-body length. This brown or gray-brown skink has 4 distinct light stripes that extend from above and below the eyes backward to the hind legs. Between the stripes on the back the scales are dark brown, and between the side stripes the scales are black. The ground color and the brown and black bands between stripes fade with age. Its tail is gray or brown. The head of the male is reddish during the breeding season.

Range Found in South Texas and the Lower Rio Grande Valley.

Habitat It is found in arid or semiarid regions with brush and grasses, as well as in wooded areas along rivers and in palm groves, where it prefers the debris formed from dead fronds.

Behavior This diurnal skink burrows under rocks or vegetative debris, often at the bases of trees. It feeds on insects and spiders.

Reproduction The female makes depressions where she lays clutches of 5 to 12 eggs from April to July. She stays with the eggs until they hatch. Hatchlings are 1½ inches or longer. They are black, and their stripes are more prominent than adults'. Their heads may be orange, and their tails are bright blue.

Ground Skink

Scincella lateralis

Description   3 to 5⅛ inches from snout to tip of long tail, which may be as much as 2½ times as long as the head and body. This small, smooth skink varies from reddish to golden brown or brown with a black dorsolateral stripe. The dorsolateral stripe extends from the eye backward onto the tail. Its belly is white or pale yellow. It has small legs and 5 toes. Its most distinctive characteristic, though difficult to use as a field mark, is a transparent window in its lower eyelid, through which it can see when the lids are closed.

Range   Found throughout the eastern half of the state and across Central Texas to the Rio Grande, including the entire coastline.

Habitat   It prefers a humid environment, usually in wooded areas with abundant leaf litter, and may be found in gardens in urban areas.

Behavior   This diurnal skink searches nervously for insects in leaf litter or rotting wood. It readily takes refuge if approached and will not hesitate to slip into nearby shallow water. When running it makes snakelike movements, probably because of its long tail.

Reproduction   It mates from January to August, and during that long breeding season it may lay up to 5 clutches of 1 to 7 eggs. The female does not stay with the eggs once she deposits them.

Gray-checkered Whiptail
Cnemidophorus dixoni

Description   8 to 12½ inches from snout to tip of tail. This long, slender lizard has 10 or 12 light dorsal stripes on a black ground color that is evenly speckled with lighter scales, giving a checkerboard effect. The throat and belly are white with no markings. The dorsal scales are small and granular, and on the belly are 8 longitudinal rows of large, smooth rectangular scales. The hips and base of the tail may be rust-colored.

Range   Found in a pocket of far West Texas in Presidio County.

Habitat   It prefers the gravelly sediment deposited by flowing water, such as in dry riverbeds or floodplains. It is usually seen in areas with sparse grasses, creosote bush, and ocotillo.

Behavior   This active, diurnal lizard forages for its insect prey in debris under low bushes. It is wary and flees readily into the nearest burrow.

Reproduction   This unisexual, all-female species reproduces by parthenogenesis, the development of unfertilized eggs. It lays eggs in June and July. Hatchlings appear about 45 days later, and their stripes are more pronounced than adults' on the checkered background.

Chihuahuan Spotted Whiptail

Cnemidophorus exsanguis

Description 9½ to 12⅜ inches from snout to tip of tail, with a long tail, up to nearly 3 times the head-body length. Six pale stripes extend from the narrow head to just behind the hips. The stripes are pale yellow to gray on the head and neck, becoming more beige posteriorly. The most conspicuous stripes are those on the sides, which may be more yellow. Between the stripes are dark fields of brown or reddish brown, and pale spots occur both in the dark fields and on the stripes. The rough tail is blue-gray to greenish, and its coloration helps distinguish this whiptail from similar species in its range. The belly is uniformly white or pale blue. As on all whiptails, the back is covered with thousands of tiny granular scales, and there are 8 rows of large rectangular scales on the belly. This lizard also has enlarged scales along the front edge of the fold on its throat and on the rear of its forelegs.

Range This lizard is found in the Trans-Pecos, but not in the Big Bend region.

Habitat Chiefly an upland lizard, its habitat varies from desert and desert grasslands to wooded mountains. It may be found in canyon bottoms, in dry washes, or on rocky hillsides, usually in areas subject to periodic flooding. It is usually seen in the open but near convenient cover.

Behavior This active lizard is diurnal and forages nervously around low bushes and in vegetative litter for its food, primarily insects.

Reproduction A unisexual, all-female species, this lizard reproduces by parthenogenesis, the development of unfertilized eggs. It lays clutches of 1 to 6 eggs from June into August, and they hatch in about 45 days. Hatchlings are about 5½ inches long, including the long tail, and their yellowish stripes are in stark contrast to the dark fields of brown or black. The characteristic light spots on stripes and in dark fields may be a pale red at hatching. According to various disparate reports, the tails of hatchlings may be blue, greenish, or orange.

Texas
Spotted
Whiptail

Cnemidophorus gularis gularis

Description   6½ to 11 inches from snout to tip of tail, with tail up to 3 times the head-body length. This brown to greenish brown lizard has 7 pale dorsal stripes from its neck to its hips. The middorsal stripe is broad and may be split, giving a count of 8 stripes. The liberal sprinkling of white or yellowish spots is most prominent on its sides. Its long tail is pinkish to orange-brown. Its back is covered with tiny granular scales, and on its belly are 8 rows of large rectangular scales. It has enlarged scales just in front of the fold on its throat and on the rear of its foreleg. Males and females differ on their ventral surfaces. The male has a reddish throat and usually some black or dark blue on the chest. It also has a dark blue belly, more uniformly blue toward the front and more speckled in back. The female has a pale pink throat and a uniformly white belly.

Range   Found throughout most of the state, excluding much of East Texas, the northern Panhandle, and the western part of the Trans-Pecos.

Habitat   Its habitat varies from arid canyon bottoms and washes to semiarid prairies. It may also be seen on rocky hillsides near floodplains and will usually be in the vicinity of a watercourse.

Behavior   This active, diurnal lizard is deliberate in its movements and not particularly wary. When approached it will dash a short distance and stop to see if it needs to keep going. It searches for food by scratching in sand or dry vegetative debris. It eats mainly termites, grasshoppers, and caterpillars but also insects and spiders.

Reproduction   It mates in April and May, and lays clutches of 1 to 5 eggs from May into June. A second clutch may be deposited in late July. Hatchlings are about 4 inches in total length, with bright light stripes and only faint spotting on the lateral dark fields. Their tails are pink or reddish, and the hips are reddish.

Plateau Spotted Whiptail

Cnemidophorus gularis septemvittatus

Description 8 to 12½ inches from snout to tip of tail, which may be as much as 3 times the head-body length. This slender lizard has 6 or 7 light dorsal stripes from its head, terminating just in front of the hips. White spots occur on the almost black or dark greenish brown fields between stripes and on the posterior of the forelegs. The hips and base of the tail, and sometimes the rear legs, are rust-colored. The rest of the tail is brown or gray in adults, blue-green in juveniles. White spots become more pronounced with age, and stripes may fade. Male and female are similar, except that the throat of the male is white and that of the female is orange. Ventral surfaces of both are white or pale bluish white. As on other whiptail lizards, the back scales are small and granular. There are 8 rows of large, smooth rectangular scales on the belly. This lizard has enlarged scales along the front edge of the fold on the throat and on the rear of the forelegs.

Range Found only in the Big Bend region.

Habitat This lizard prefers a rocky habitat with sparse vegetation and may be found in desert foothills or in the mountains.

Behavior This diurnal lizard is less nervous than other whiptails, and its movements are slow and deliberate when it is searching for its insect prey. It may root in vegetative litter to uncover insects, possibly indicating well-developed hearing and sense of smell.

Reproduction It mates in late spring and lays eggs in midsummer. Hatchlings are about 4½ inches long, including the long blue or greenish tail. The 6 or 7 light stripes are usually wavy, with the middorsal stripe broken irregularly down its length. The fields between stripes are darker than in adults. The only light spots occur on the lateral dark field.

Trans-Pecos Striped Whiptail

Cnemidophorus inornatus heptagrammus

Description   6½ to 9⅜ inches from snout to tip of tail, with tail up to 3 times the length of the head and body. The most outstanding field marks on this slender lizard are its bright blue tail and the blue on the sides of its head. It has 6 to 8 light stripes separated by dark grayish or nearly black unspotted fields. The light stripes extend from the head onto the tail before disappearing where the tail becomes blue. The throat and belly are blue, darker blue on the male and bluish white on the female. The back is covered with thousands of small granular scales, and the belly has 8 rows of large, smooth rectangular scales. The scales on the front edge of the fold on the throat are enlarged, as are 2 rows of scales on the posterior of the forelegs.

Range   Found throughout the Trans-Pecos, including the Big Bend region.

Habitat   In both arid and semiarid regions, this lizard prefers rocky slopes or flatlands with scattered vegetation. It may also be found in areas with sandy silt deposited by periodic flooding.

Behavior   This wary diurnal lizard eats beetles, grasshoppers, and spiders. When approached it will retreat to the nearest shrub cover but will move on to a convenient burrow if pursued.

Reproduction   It mates in spring and lays 2 to 4 eggs from May to July. Hatchlings are about 3⅜ inches long, and the pale stripes are yellowish on black fields. The ventral surfaces are paler blue than on adults.

Laredo Striped Whiptail

Cnemidophorus laredoensis

Description 6 to 11⁵⁄₁₆ inches from snout to tip of long rough tail. This slender lizard has 7 light stripes extending from its head onto its greenish brown tail. The stripes are separated by dark green or greenish brown fields. It may have small, indistinct light spots on the lateral dark fields. The middorsal stripe may be narrower than others and may be broken irregularly. As on other whiptails, the scales on its back are small and granular, and there are 8 rows of large, smooth rectangular scales on its belly.

Range Found from Webb County to Starr County along the Rio Grande.

Habitat This lizard lives in a semiarid region with only sparse vegetation. It usually is found near streambeds at the bases of hills.

Behavior This active diurnal lizard feeds on a variety of insects. It may root or dig in debris or soil for its prey.

Reproduction A unisexual, all-female species, this lizard reproduces by parthenogenesis, the development of unfertilized eggs. It deposits one or more clutches of 1 to 4 eggs in June and July, and they hatch in July and August. Juveniles are similar to adults.

Marbled Whiptail

Cnemidophorus marmoratus

Description 8 to 12 inches from snout to tip of tail, with tail about 2½ to 3 times the head-body length. The marbled whiptail is so named because its pattern of 4 to 8 indistinct light stripes and covering of light and dark spots on a gray ground color create a marbled effect. Its sides are usually patterned with alternating light and dark bars, hence the scientific species name referring to the tiger. The dorsal stripes and spots may be faded, leaving a gray, patternless appearance, especially in individuals on the eastern edge of the range. The tail is gray or gray-green with flecks of black along the sides and dark on the underside. The ventral surfaces are white or pale yellow, with a pale peach color on the throat, extending to the chest and sides on mature individuals. The chin, throat, and chest may have some black flecks, and in some rare individuals the ventral surfaces may be all black. Typical of whiptails, this lizard has small granular scales on its back. On its belly there are 8 longitudinal rows of large, smooth rectangular scales. The scales just in front of the fold on the throat are slightly enlarged, but they are separated from the fold by a row of granular scales. There are no enlarged scales on the rear of the forelegs.

Range Found throughout the Trans-Pecos, including the Big Bend region. Isolated populations are found in South Texas around Laredo and in a sandy region at the base of the Panhandle, east of Lubbock.

Habitat This lizard prefers sandy areas where vegetation is sparse, allowing room for running. It is found in arid and semi-arid locations and in open wooded areas.

Behavior This diurnal lizard is likely to be active even on very hot days. It moves about continuously in search of prey and may dig burrows to unearth insects. It also eats scorpions and spiders. It is extremely wary, and if approached it will dash from one clump of vegetation to another some distance away. It will eventually disappear down a burrow, which may be of its own making. It stalks moving prey and may even stalk vegetative litter swaying in the breeze.

Reproduction   Mating occurs in April and May. It lays clutches of 1 to 4 eggs in May and sometimes a second clutch in July. Hatchlings emerge in July and August. They are patterned with many small pale spots or dashes in longitudinal rows on a dark brown to black ground color. Their tails are bright blue.

New Mexico Whiptail

Cnemidophorus neomexicanus

Description   8 to 11⅞ inches from snout to tip of long tail, which may be slightly more than 3 times the head-body length. This slender lizard has 7 pale yellow stripes separated by dark brown to black fields with indistinct light spots. The middorsal stripe is wavy and forks on the top of the head. The tail is gray at the base, changing to green or greenish blue. The throat is pale blue or blue-green, and the belly is white or pale blue and has 8 rows of large, smooth rectangular scales. The scales on the back are uniformly small and granular.

Range   Found in the extreme western tip of the state and along the westernmost course of the Rio Grande.

Habitat   This lizard prefers sandy areas with sparse grasses where periodic flooding occurs, such as in washes, river beaches, and bottoms. It seems to be at home in areas disturbed by human activity, such as along fencerows or near trash piles.

Behavior   This active diurnal lizard forages for its insect prey in vegetative debris and trash piles. If disturbed, it takes shelter under nearby debris.

Reproduction   A unisexual, all-female species, it reproduces by parthenogenesis, the development of unfertilized eggs. It lays small clutches of 2 to 4 eggs in summer, and the eggs hatch in 50 to 60 days. Hatchlings are about 5 inches long, including the bright blue tail. They are strongly striped with yellow on black, light-spotted fields.

Six-lined Racerunner

Cnemidophorus sexlineatus sexlineatus

Description   6 to 9½ inches from snout to tip of slender tail, which may be 2⅓ times the head-body length. This slender lizard has 6 light yellow, white, or gray stripes extending from just behind the eyes down the body; they are most prominent on the sides. The dorsolateral stripes continue onto the tail. Between the stripes, the fields are dark greenish brown to almost black and unspotted. There may be a light beige stripe down the mid-dorsal line onto the tail. Male and female are similar, but the stripes on the male may be less distinct. The throat on the male is pale green and the belly is pale blue. The female is white on all ventral surfaces. The hind legs on both sexes are long and sturdy. The scales just in front of the deep fold on the throat are dramatically enlarged, but the scales on the rear of the forelegs are usually not enlarged. There are 8 rows of large, smooth rectangular scales on the belly.

Range   Found throughout East Texas and to the south about halfway down the coastline.

Habitat   It inhabits a variety of terrains, preferring open areas with well-drained sand or loose soil. It may also be found in or near woods and on floodplains.

Behavior   This diurnal lizard is very active, especially in the morning. It is speedy and when approached will take refuge in vegetative litter or under rocks. It seeks shelter from cool temperatures in burrows, probably digging burrows for itself. It is bold in foraging for its insect prey.

Reproduction   It mates from April to June and lays clutches of 1 to 6 eggs from June to July. A second clutch may be deposited 3 weeks after the first. Eggs hatch from June into September, and hatchlings are about 2¾ inches long, including the slender blue tail. The light stripes on juveniles are yellow and contrast sharply with the nearly black fields.

Prairie-lined Racerunner

Cnemidophorus sexlineatus viridis

Description   6 to 10½ inches from snout to tip of slender tail, with tail up to 2⅓ times the head-body length. Females may be a little larger than males. This lizard has 7 light stripes on a bright green head and body. The stripes extend from just behind the eye down the body and are most prominent on the sides. The dorsolateral stripes extend onto the tail, which is brown. The fields between stripes are unspotted. There may be a beige stripe down the middorsal line extending onto the tail. Male and female are similarly patterned on the dorsum, but the belly of the male is pale blue and that of the female is white. The dorsal scales on both are granular, and there are 8 rows of large, smooth rectangular scales on the belly. The scales just in front of the deep fold on the throat are dramatically enlarged, but those on the rear of the foreleg are not usually enlarged. Hind legs on both sexes are long and sturdy.

Range   Found in a wide wedge down the center of the state, from the Panhandle to the Lower Rio Grande Valley.

Habitat   Found in a variety of habitats, it prefers dry sunny areas, such as the banks and floodplains of rivers, open grassy areas, and rocky outcroppings. It may also be found on lowlands and hilly terrains.

Behavior   This diurnal lizard is very active, especially in the morning. It is speedy and when approached will take refuge in vegetative litter or under rocks. It seeks shelter from cool temperatures in burrows, probably digging burrows for itself. It is bold in foraging for its insect prey.

Reproduction   It mates from April to June and lays clutches of 1 to 6 eggs from June to July. A second clutch may be deposited 3 weeks after the first. Eggs hatch from June into September, and hatchlings are about 2¾ inches long, including the slender blue tail. The light stripes on juveniles are yellow and contrast sharply with the separating fields.

Colorado Checkered Whiptail

Cnemidophorus tesselatus

Description   11 to 15½ inches from snout to tip of tail, with tail up to nearly 3 times as long as the head and body. This largest of the whiptail lizards in Texas varies in color and pattern from one individual to another. Generally, this slender lizard has black spots or bars on a creamy yellow field, giving the appearance of checks. It may have 6 indistinct light stripes. Spotting is not distinct in some populations. The long, sturdy hind legs may be boldly spotted, with light spots on a black field, and the forelegs and sides of the head may have black spots on a light field. The tail is yellow or brown with spots on the sides only. The throat and belly are white, and there may be small flecks of black on the chin and chest. The dorsal scales are small and granular, and there are 8 longitudinal rows of large, smooth rectangular scales on the belly. The scales just in front of the fold on the throat are much larger than those around them, but there are usually no enlarged scales on the rear of the forelegs.

Range   Found throughout the Trans-Pecos, including the Big Bend region, and in the western part of the Panhandle.

Habitat   This lizard is at home in a variety of habitats but almost always in association with rocky areas. It may be seen on open plains, in canyons, into foothills, and along the Rio Grande floodplains.

Behavior   This diurnal lizard is a skillful rock climber. It eats scorpions, insects, and spiders. It seems to prefer living in small groups isolated from each other. It is less wary than other whiptails, often allowing close approach.

Reproduction   This unisexual, all-female species reproduces by parthenogenesis, the development of unfertilized eggs. Eggs are deposited from June into July in clutches of 2 to 8, and they hatch in August. Hatchlings may be up to 4 inches long, including the tail. They are patterned with 6 light stripes, sometimes more, on dark fields with pale spots. The middorsal light stripe may be broken into dots or dashes and appear wavy.

Desert Grassland Whiptail

Cnemidophorus uniparens

Description   6½ to 9⅜ inches from snout to tip of tail, with tail 2½ times the head-body length. This small, slender lizard has 6 distinct light stripes separated by fields of reddish brown to black. It has no spots. There is usually a suggestion of a seventh stripe down the middorsal line, especially apparent on the neck. The stripes on the back are yellow, and those on the sides are paler, almost white. The tail is olive-green. The ventral surfaces are white and usually unmarked. In adults the chin and sides of neck may appear bluish. The back scales are small and granular, and there are 8 longitudinal rows of large, smooth rectangular scales on the belly. The scales along the front edge of the fold on the throat are enlarged, and there are enlarged scales on the rear of the forelegs.

Range   Found in a small area in the extreme western tip of the state.

Habitat   This lizard prefers low arid and semiarid desert areas with some vegetation. It also inhabits lower mountainous areas and river valleys.

Behavior   This diurnal lizard is active and prowls in search of its insect prey.

Reproduction   A unisexual, all-female species, it reproduces by parthenogenesis, the development of unfertilized eggs. It lays 1 to 4 eggs during the summer, and they hatch in 50 to 55 days. Hatchlings are about 3 inches long, including the blue tail.

Appendix 1:
Collecting Texas
Amphibians and Reptiles

In the state of Texas, it is illegal to collect amphibians and reptiles unless you have a valid Texas hunting license. In addition, certain species are protected. Special permission must be obtained from the Parks and Wildlife Department before such species are collected or killed. The following list of protected species, designated as threatened or endangered, was current as of April 1987 but is subject to revision. It is always advisable to contact the Parks and Wildlife Department if in doubt. Such information is available at this address:

Texas Parks and Wildlife Department
4200 Smith School Road
Austin, TX 78744

THREATENED AMPHIBIANS
Mexican treefrog *Smilisca baudinii*
Sheep frog *Hypopachus variolosus*
Mexican burrowing toad *Rhinophrynus dorsalis*
San Marcos salamander *Eurycea nana*
Comal blind salamander *Eurycea tridentifera*

THREATENED REPTILES
Common green turtle *Chelonia mydas*
Alligator snapping turtle *Macroclemys temminckii*
Texas tortoise *Gopherus berlandieri*
Reticulated gecko *Coleonyx reticulatus*
Reticulate collared lizard *Crotaphytus reticulatus*
Texas horned lizard *Phrynosoma cornutum*
Mountain short-horned lizard *Phrynosoma douglassii hernandesi*

ENDANGERED AMPHIBIANS
Houston toad *Bufo houstonensis*
White-lipped frog *Leptodactylus fragilis*
Texas blind salamander *Typhlomolge rathbuni*
Blanco blind salamander *Typhlomolge robusta*
Black-spotted newt *Notophthalmus meridionalis*
Rio Grande lesser siren *Siren intermedia texana*

ENDANGERED REPTILES
Loggerhead turtle *Caretta caretta*
Atlantic hawksbill turtle *Eretmochelys imbricata imbricata*
Kemp's Ridley turtle *Lepidochelys kempi*
Leatherback turtle *Dermochelys coriacea*
Mexican plateau mud turtle *Kinosternon hirtipes murrayi*

Appendix 2:
Photo Information

The purpose of this appendix is to provide the locality data of the animals in the photographs. Locality is listed as state:county in most cases; foreign localities are given as country:state. Mention is made, in the case of a few photos, when particular characteristics of sex or age are illustrated. Whenever possible, photographs of Texas animals were used in the illustration of this field guide. Many photographed animals were placed in the University of Texas at Arlington Collection of Vertebrates as voucher specimens. The museum numbers of such specimens are listed in this appendix, and these specimens are available for examination upon request to the Museum of Herpetology, Department of Biology, University of Texas at Arlington.

TOADS AND FROGS
Toads: Family Bufonidae

Dwarf American toad *Bufo americanus charlesmithi*
OK:Leflore
UTA-A-20003

Great Plains toad *Bufo cognatus*
TX:Swisher
UTA-A-15898

Eastern green toad *Bufo debilis debilis*
TX:Somervell
UTA-A-19986

Western green toad *Bufo debilis insidior*
NM:Luna

Houston toad *Bufo houstonensis*
TX:Bastrop

Giant toad *Bufo marinus*
A. TX:Starr
UTA-A-17419
B. TX:Starr
UTA-A-17421
recently metamorphosed juvenile

Red-spotted toad *Bufo punctatus*
TX:Val Verde
UTA-A-19866

Texas toad *Bufo speciosus*
TX:Val Verde

Gulf Coast toad *Bufo valliceps valliceps*
TX:Jasper
UTA-A-18690

East Texas toad *Bufo velatus*
A. TX:Jasper
   UTA-A-18691
B. TX:Jasper
   UTA-A-18692

Southwestern Woodhouse's toad *Bufo woodhouseii australis*
NM:Luna

Woodhouse's toad *Bufo woodhouseii woodhouseii*
TX:Dallas

Treefrogs and relatives: Family Hylidae

Blanchard's cricket frog *Acris crepitans blanchardi*
A. TX:Llano
B. TX:Llano

Northern cricket frog *Acris crepitans crepitans*
OK:McCurtain
UTA-A-18580

Coastal cricket frog *Acris crepitans paludicola*
no photo

Canyon treefrog *Hyla arenicolor*
MX:Sonora
UTA-A-20256

Cope's gray treefrog *Hyla chrysoscelis*
TX:Llano
UTA-A-17568

Green treefrog *Hyla cinerea*
TX:Anderson
UTA-A-19159

Squirrel treefrog *Hyla squirella*
A. TX:Orange
B. TX:Orange
   UTA-A-17561

Gray treefrog *Hyla versicolor*
TX:Anderson
UTA-A-19190

Spotted chorus frog *Pseudacris clarkii*
TX:Tarrant
UTA-A-18427

Northern spring peeper *Pseudacris crucifer crucifer*
TX:Anderson
UTA-A-19162

Strecker's chorus frog *Pseudacris streckeri streckeri*
A. TX:Somervell
   UTA-A-17964
B. TX:Tarrant
   UTA-A-18437

Upland chorus frog *Pseudacris triseriata feriarum*
TX:Anderson

Mexican treefrog *Smilisca baudinii*
TX:Cameron
UTA-A-21055

Tropical Frogs: Family Leptodactylidae

Eastern barking frog *Hylactophryne augusti latrans*
MX:Jalisco
UTA-A-12982

White-lipped frog *Leptodactylus fragilis*
no data

Rio Grande chirping frog *Syrrhophus cystignathoides campi*
TX:Cameron

Spotted chirping frog *Syrrhophus guttilatus*
TX:Brewster
UTA-A-19998

Cliff chirping frog *Syrrhophus marnockii*
TX:Hays
UTA-A-19499

Narrowmouth Toads: Family Microhylidae

Eastern narrowmouth toad *Gastrophryne carolinensis*
A. TX:Orange
   UTA-A-17617
B. TX:Anderson
   UTA-A-19200

Great Plains narrowmouth toad *Gastrophryne olivacea*
A. TX:Hays
   UTA-A-19512
B. TX:Somervell
   UTA-A-17619

Sheep frog *Hypopachus variolosus*
TX:Starr

Spadefoot Toads: Family Pelobatidae

Plains spadefoot *Scaphiopus bombifrons*
A. no data
B. TX:Swisher
   UTA-A-15892

Couch's spadefoot *Scaphiopus couchii*
TX:Knox
UTA-A-15895

Hurter's spadefoot *Scaphiopus holbrookii hurterii*
A. TX:Jasper
   UTA-A-17741
B. TX:Anderson
   UTA-A-19130

Southern spadefoot *Scaphiopus multiplicatus*
TX:Swisher
UTA-A-15896

True Frogs: Family Ranidae

Southern crawfish frog *Rana areolata areolata*
TX:Anderson
UTA-A-19204

Rio Grande leopard frog *Rana berlandieri*
TX:Starr
UTA-A-17631

Plains leopard frog *Rana blairi*
TX:Haskell
UTA-A-15902

Bull frog *Rana catesbeiana*
A. TX:Frio
   UTA-A-17649
   male
B. TX:Henderson
   UTA-A-19871
   female

Bronze frog *Rana clamitans clamitans*
TX:Orange
UTA-A-17660

Pig frog *Rana grylio*
no data

Pickerel frog *Rana palustris*
TX:Wood
UTA-A-17932

Southern leopard frog *Rana sphenocephala*
TX:Freestone
UTA-A-18484

Mexican Burrowing Toad: Family Rhinophrynidae

Mexican burrowing toad *Rhinophrynus dorsalis*
TX:Starr

SALAMANDERS

Mole Salamanders: Family Ambystomatidae

Spotted salamander *Ambystoma maculatum*
TX

Marbled salamander *Ambystoma opacum*
TX:Jasper
UTA-A-9128

Mole salamander *Ambystoma talpoideum*
MS:Madison

Smallmouth salamander *Ambystoma texanum*
TX:Hunt

Barred tiger salamander *Ambystoma tigrinum mavortium*
TX:

Eastern tiger salamander *Ambystoma tigrinum tigrinum*
TX:

Amphiumas: Family Amphiumidae

Three-toed amphiuma *Amphiuma tridactylum*
TX:Smith

Mudpuppies: Family Proteidae

Gulf Coast waterdog *Necturus beyeri*
TX:Cherokee
UTA-A-Lire collection

Lungless Salamanders: Family Plethodontidae

Southern dusky salamander *Desmognathus auriculatus*
UTA-A-18485

Cascade Caverns salamander *Eurycea latitans*
TX:Kendall

San Marcos salamander *Eurycea nana*
TX:Hays

Texas salamander *Eurycea neotenes*
TX:Comal

Dwarf salamander *Eurycea quadridigitata*
TX:Jasper
UTA-A-18032

Comal blind salamander *Eurycea tridentifera*
TX:Bexar

Valdina Farms salamander *Eurycea troglodytes*
TX:Medina

Whitethroat slimy salamander *Plethodon glutinosus albagula*
TX:Hays
UTA-A-19496

Slimy salamander *Plethodon glutinosus glutinosus*
OK

Southern redback salamander *Plethodon serratus*
OK:McCurtain

Texas blind salamander *Typhlomolge rathbuni*
TX:Hays

Blanco blind salamander *Typhlomolge robusta*
no photo

Newts: Family Salamandridae

Black-spotted newt *Notophthalmus meridionalis*
TX:Cameron

Central newt *Notophthalmus viridescens louisianensis*
A. TX:Anderson
   UTA-A-19124
   adult
B. TX:Jasper
   UTA-A-17708
   eft stage

Sirens: Family Sirenidae

Western lesser siren *Siren intermedia nettingi*
juvenile

Rio Grande lesser siren *Siren intermedia texana*
TX:Cameron

TURTLES

Marine Turtles: Family Cheloniidae

Loggerhead turtle *Caretta caretta*
no photo
Common green turtle *Chelonia mydas*
no data

Atlantic hawksbill turtle *Eretmochelys imbricata imbricata*
Costa Rica:Tortuguero
Kemp's Ridley turtle *Lepidochelys kempi*
no data

Snapping Turtles: Family Chelydridae
Common snapping turtle *Chelydra serpentina serpentina*
no data
Alligator snapping turtle *Macroclemys temminckii*
TX:Smith
UTA-R-14690

Leatherback turtles: Family Dermochelyidae
Leatherback turtle *Dermochelys coriacea*
French Guiana

Water Turtles and Box Turtles: Family Emydidae
Western painted turtle *Chrysemys picta belli*
OK
Southern painted turtle *Chrysemys picta dorsalis*
OK
Western chicken turtle *Deirochelys reticularia miaria*
TX:Tarrant
UTA-R-17287
Cagle's map turtle *Graptemys caglei*
A. TX:Dewitt
B. TX:Dewitt
Ouachita map turtle *Graptemys ouachitensis ouachitensis*
OK
Sabine map turtle *Graptemys ouachitensis sabinensis*
TX:Panola
UTA-R-17046
Mississippi map turtle *Graptemys pseudogeographica kohnii*
A. TX:Red River
   UTA-R-17503, female
B. TX:Smith
   UTA-R-16623
   male
Texas map turtle *Graptemys versa*
TX
Texas diamondback terrapin *Malaclemys terrapin littoralis*
TX: San Patricio

Rio Grande cooter *Pseudemys concinna gorzugi*
no photo

Metter's river cooter *Pseudemys concinna metteri*
TX:Bosque

Texas cooter *Pseudemys texana*
TX:Tarrant

Three-toed box turtle *Terrapene carolina triunguis*
TX:Kaufman

Ornate box turtle *Terrapene ornata ornata*
TX:Freestone

Desert box turtle *Terrapene ornata luteola*
AZ:Cochise

Big Bend slider *Trachemys gaigeae*
TX:Brewster

Red-eared slider *Trachemys scripta elegans*
TX:Bosque
hatchling

Mud and Musk Turtles: Family Kinosternidae

Yellow mud turtle *Kinosternon flavescens flavescens*
TX:Tarrant
UTA-R-17285

Mexican Plateau mud turtle *Kinosternon hirtipes murrayi*
MX:Chihuahua
UTA-R-17928

Mississippi mud turtle *Kinosternon subrubrum hippocrepis*
TX:Orange
UTA-R-17772

Razorback musk turtle *Sternotherus carinatus*
TX:Tarrant
UTA-R-17052

Common musk turtle *Sternotherus odoratus*
OK

Tortoises: Family Testudinidae

Texas tortoise *Gopherus berlandieri*
TX:Starr

Softshell turtles: Family Trionichidae

Midland smooth softshell *Trionyx muticus muticus*
KS

Texas spiny softshell *Trionyx spiniferus emoryi*
TX:Cameron

Guadalupe spiny softshell *Trionyx spiniferus guadalupensis*
TX:DeWitt

Western spiny softshell *Trionyx spiniferus hartwegi*
KS

Pallid spiny softshell *Trionyx spiniferus pallidus*
TX:Tarrant

CROCODILIANS
Crocodilians: Family Crocodylidae

American alligator *Alligator mississippiensis*
A. TX:Henderson
juvenile
B. Spectacled caiman *Caiman crocodilus*
no data

LIZARDS
Anguid Lizards: Family Anguidae

Texas alligator lizard *Gerrhonotus liocephalus infernalis*
TX:Bexar

Western slender glass lizard *Ophisaurus attenuatus attenuatus*
TX:Henderson
UTA-R-16927

Geckos: Family Gekkonidae

Texas banded gecko *Coleonyx brevis*
TX:Val Verde
UTA-R-17035

Reticulated gecko *Coleonyx reticulatus*
TX:Brewster

Bent-toed gecko *Cyrtodactylus scaber*
no photo

Mediterranean gecko *Hemidactylus turcicus*
TX:Starr

Iguanid Lizards: Family Iguanidae

Green anole *Anolis carolinensis*
TX:Jasper

Brown anole *Anolis sagrei*
no data

Southwest earless lizard *Cophosaurus texanus scitulus*
TX:Brewster
Texas earless lizard *Cophosaurus texanus texanus*
TX:Johnson
Eastern collared lizard *Crotaphytus collaris collaris*
A. TX:Wise
UTA-R-14827
male
B. TX:Wise
UTA-R-15322
female
Chihuahuan collared lizard *Crotaphytus collaris fuscus*
MX:Sonora
UTA-R-17342
Reticulate collared lizard *Crotaphytus reticulatus*
TX:Zapata
Broad-ringed spiny-tailed iguana *Ctenosaura pectinata*
no photo
Longnose leopard lizard *Gambelia wislizenii wislizenii*
no data
Plateau earless lizard *Holbrookia lacerata lacerata*
no photo
Southern earless lizard *Holbrookia lacerata subcaudalis*
no photo
Speckled earless lizard *Holbrookia maculata approximans*
no photo
Northern earless lizard *Holbrookia maculata maculata*
A. MX:Sonora
UTA-R-17346
B. MX:Sonora
UTA-R-17349
gravid female
Eastern earless lizard *Holbrookia maculata perspicua*
no photo
Keeled earless lizard *Holbrookia propinqua propinqua*
TX:Cameron
UTA-R-14869
male
Texas horned lizard *Phrynosoma cornutum*
TX:McMullen
UTA-R-17077

Mountain short-horned lizard *Phrynosoma douglassii hernandesi*
NM:Gila National Forest

Roundtail horned lizard *Phrynosoma modestum*
TX:Val Verde

Blue spiny lizard *Sceloporus cyanogenys*
TX:Starr
UTA-R-14944
young male

Dunes sagebrush lizard *Sceloporus graciosus arenicolous*
TX:Ward
UTA-R-19497

Mesquite lizard *Sceloporus grammicus microlepidotus*
TX:Starr
UTA-R-14954

Twin-spotted spiny lizard *Sceloporus magister bimaculosus*
TX:Presidio
UTA-R-16177

Big Bend canyon lizard *Sceloporus merriami annulatus*
TX:Brewster
UTA-R-17244

Presidio canyon lizard *Sceloporus merriami longipunctatus*
A. TX:Presidio
   male
B. TX:Presido
   male, belly pattern

Merriam's canyon lizard *Sceloporus merriami merriami*
TX:Val Verde

Texas spiny lizard *Sceloporus olivaceus*
A. TX:Tarrant
   UTA-R-11139
B. TX:Hidalgo
   UTA-R-15583
   female

Crevice spiny lizard *Sceloporus poinsettii poinsettii*
TX:El Paso

Southern prairie lizard *Sceloporus undulatus consobrinus*
TX:Erath
UTA-R-15070

Northern prairie lizard *Sceloporus undulatus garmani*
TX:Hutchinson

Northern fence lizard *Sceloporus undulatus hyacinthinus*
A. TX:Jasper
   UTA-R-16888
B. TX:Jasper
   UTA-R-16889

Rosebelly lizard *Sceloporus variabilis marmoratus*
TX:Hidalgo
UTA-R-15086

Eastern tree lizard *Urosaurus ornatus ornatus*
TX:Llano
UTA-R-11110

Big Bend tree lizard *Urosaurus ornatus schmidti*
A. TX:Jeff Davis
   UTA-R-17261
   male
B. TX:Jeff Davis
   UTA-R-17261
   male, belly pattern

Desert side-blotched lizard *Uta stansburiana stejnegeri*
TX:Ward
UTA-R-15165

Skinks: Family Scincidae

Southern coal skink *Eumeces anthracinus pluvialis*
OK:McCurtain
UTA-R-16269

Five-lined skink *Eumeces faciatus*
A. TX:Freestone
   UTA-R-15303
   juvenile
B. TX:Jasper
   UTA-R-17272
   adult male

Broadhead skink *Eumeces laticeps*
TX:Tarrant
adult male

Variable skink *Eumeces multivirgatus epipleurotus*
TX:Brewster

Great Plains skink *Eumeces obsoletus*
A. TX:Swisher
   UTA-R-17274
   adult male

B. TX:Swisher
   UTA-R-17275
   juvenile

Southern prairie skink *Eumeces septentrionalis obtusirostris*
TX:Tarrant
UTA-R-15347

Short-lined skink *Eumeces tetragrammus brevilineatus*
TX:Llano

Four-lined skink *Eumeces tetragrammus tetragrammus*
TX:Frio
UTA-15591

Ground skink *Scincella lateralis*
TX:Llano

Whiptails: Family Teiidae

Gray-checkered whiptail *Cnemidophorus dixoni*
no photo

Chihuahuan spotted whiptail *Cnemidophorus exsanguis*
TX:Jeff Davis
UTA-R-17280

Texas spotted whiptail *Cnemidophorus gularis gularis*
TX:Tarrant
adult male

Plateau spotted whiptail *Cnemidophorus gularis septemvittatus*
TX:Brewster
UTA-R-17282

Trans-Pecos striped whiptail *Cnemidophorus inornatus heptagrammus*
TX:Brewster
UTA-R-17675

Laredo striped whiptail *Cnemidophorus laredoensis*
TX:Starr
UTA-R-14932

Marbled whiptail *Cnemidophorus marmoratus*
TX:Brewster

New Mexico whiptail *Cnemidophorus neomexicanus*
no photo

Six-lined racerunner *Cnemidophorus sexlineatus sexlineatus*
no data

Prairie-lined racerunner *Cnemidophorus sexlineatus viridis*
TX:Parker
UTA-R-17124

Colorado checkered whiptail *Cnemidophorus tesselatus*
TX:Culberson
Desert grassland whiptail *Cnemidophorus uniparens*
NM:Luna

Glossary

amphipod A small crustacean.

anterior Near the head or front.

arboreal Living in trees.

axillary Related to or near the armpit.

barbel A slender, fleshy, whiskerlike projection on the chin and throat of turtles.

boss A rounded protuberance on top of the head and between the eyes of some toads.

bridge On a turtle's shell, a distinct segment connecting the upper and lower parts.

carapace The upper part of a turtle's shell.

copepod A small crustacean found in either seawater or fresh water.

costal grooves Vertical grooves on the sides of salamanders between the front and back legs.

cranial crest A bony ridge between or behind the eyes on some toads.

dewlap A vertical fold of skin on the throat of some lizards.

diurnal Active during the daytime.

dorsal Pertaining to the back or upper surface.

dorsolateral Pertaining to an area between the middle of the back and the side.

dorsum The back or upper surface.

eft The terrestrial life stage of the newt.

gravid Pregnant with eggs or young.

keel A longitudinal ridge on the upper or lower shell of some turtles. Also, a ridge along the back and tail of some salamanders.

keeled scale A scale with a longitudinal ridge.

marginal An enlarged scale on the periphery of a turtle shell.

metamorphose To change in form and habits from a larva to an adult.

middorsal Pertaining to the middle of the back.

midventral Pertaining to the middle of the belly.

omnivorous Eating all kinds of food, animal and vegetable.

parotoid gland An external gland on the shoulders of toads just behind the eyes.

parthenogenesis Reproduction without fertilization of the female.

plastron The lower shell of the turtle.

posterior Near the rear of the body, or behind.

postlabial Behind the mouth.

prehensile   Adapted for wrapping around or holding.

resaca   A quiet body of water isolated by a change in the Rio Grande's course.

reticulated   Having a netlike pattern.

scute   An enlarged scale on a turtle's shell.

spade   An enlarged tubercle on the underside of a toad's hind foot, used for digging.

supralabial   Above the mouth.

terrestrial   Land-dwelling.

truncated   Appearing abruptly shortened.

tubercle   A small rounded projection; a wart.

tympanum   The eardrum. On toads and frogs, it is a round, smooth structure on each side of the head, behind the eye.

ventral   Pertaining to the undersurface.

vestigial   Remaining in a rudimentary form.

vocal sac   An inflatable pouch on the throat of male frogs and toads, which use it to produce resonance when calling.

Bibliography of Works Consulted

Axtell, Ralph W. "*Eumeces epipleurotus* Cope, a Revived Name for the Southwestern Skink *Eumeces multivirgatus gaigei* Taylor." *The Texas Journal of Science,* Vol. XIII, No. 2 (June 1961), pp. 345–351.

Behler, John L., and F. Wayne King. *The Audubon Society Field Guide to North American Reptiles and Amphibians.* New York: Alfred A. Knopf, 1979.

Bloom, Roy A., Kyle W. Selcer, and W. Ken King. "Status of the Introduced Gekkonid Lizard, *Cyrtodactylus scaber,* in Galveston, Texas." *The Southwestern Naturalist,* Vol. 31, No. 1 (March 1986), pp. 129–131.

Burger, W. Leslie, Philip W. Smith, and Hobart M. Smith. "Notable Records of Reptiles and Amphibians in Oklahoma, Arkansas, and Texas." *Journal of the Tennessee Academy of Science,* 1949, pp. 130–134.

Collins, Joseph T., et al. *Standard Common and Current Scientific Names for North American Amphibians and Reptiles.* Lawrence, Kan.: Society for the Study of Amphibians and Reptiles, 1982.

Conant, Roger. *A Field Guide to Reptiles and Amphibians of Eastern and Central North America,* 2nd ed. Boston: Houghton Mifflin, 1975.

Dixon, James R. *Amphibians and Reptiles of Texas.* College Station: Texas A&M University Press, 1987.

"Hawksbill Turtle." National Fish and Wildlife Laboratory, the Office of Endangered Species and the National Coastal Ecosystems Team, Office of Biological Services, March 1980 (FWS/OBS/01.22).

Hedges, S. Blair. "An Electrophoretic Analysis of Holarctic Hylid Frog Evolution." *Systematic Zoology,* Vol. 35, No. 1 (March 1986), pp. 1–21.

Iverson, John. *Checklist of the Turtles of the World With English Common Names.* Society for the Study of Amphibians and Reptiles, Herpetological Circular No. 14, 1985.

"Kemp's (Atlantic) Ridley Sea Turtle." National Fish and Wildlife Laboratory, the Office of Endangered Species and the National Coastal Ecosystems Team, Office of Biological Services, March 1980 (FWS/OBS/01.30).

Leviton, Alan E. *Reptiles and Amphibians of North America.* New York: Doubleday, 1972.

Lieb, Carl S. "Systematics and Distribution of the Skinks Allied to *Eumeces tetragrammus* (Sauria: Scincidae)." Natural History Museum of Los Angeles County, Contributions in Science No. 357. Los Angeles: April 11, 1985.

Mecham, John S. "The Taxonomic Status of Some Southwestern Skinks of the *multivirgatus* Group." *Copeia,* 1957(2), pp. 111–123.

Morris, Percy A. *An Introduction to the Reptiles and Amphibians of the United States.* New York: Dover, 1974. (Originally published 1944, Lancaster, Pa.: The Jacques Cattell Press.)

Murphy, Robert W., and R. C. Drewes. "Comments on the Occurrence of *Smilisca baudini* (Dumeril and Bibron) (Amphibia: Hylidae) in Bexar County, Texas." *The Texas Journal of Science,* Vol. XXVII, No. 3 (September 1976), pp. 406–407.

Potter, Floyd E., Jr., and Samuel S. Sweet. "Generic Boundaries in Texas Cave Salamanders, and a Redescription of *Typhlomolge robusta* (Amphibia: Plethodontidae)." *Copeia,* 1981(1), pp. 64–75.

Raun, Gerald G., and Frederick R. Gehlbach. *Amphibians and Reptiles in Texas.* The Dallas Natural Science Association and the Dallas Museum of Natural History, Bulletin 2. Dallas: 1972.

Seidel, Michael E., and Hobart M. Smith. "*Chrysemys, Pseudemys, Trachemys* (Testudines: Emydidae) Did Agassiz Have It Right?" *Herpetologica,* 42(2), 1986, pp. 242–248.

Selcer, Kyle W., and Roy A. Bloom. "*Cyrtodactylus scaber* (Gekkonidae): A New Gecko to the Fauna of the United States." *The Southwestern Naturalist,* Vol. 29, No. 4 (November 1984), pp. 499–500.

Smith, Hobart M. *Handbook of Lizards: Lizards of the United States and of Canada,* 3rd ed. Ithaca, New York: Comstock, 1946.

———, and Edmund D. Brodie, Jr. *A Guide to Field Identification: Reptiles of North America.* New York: Golden Press, 1982.

Smith, Malcolm A. *The Fauna of British India, Including Ceylon and Burma, Vol. II—Sauria.* London: Taylor and Francis, 1935.

Stebbins, Robert C. *Amphibians and Reptiles of Western North America,* 6th ed. New York: McGraw-Hill, 1954.

———. *A Field Guide to Western Reptiles and Amphibians.* Boston: Houghton Mifflin, 1966.

———. *A Field Guide to Western Reptiles and Amphibians,* 2nd ed., rev. Boston: Houghton Mifflin, 1985.

Sweet, Samuel S. "Secondary Contact and Hybridization in the Texas Cave Salamanders *Eurycea neotenes* and *E. tridentifera.*" *Copeia,* 1984(2), pp. 428–441.

Ward, Joseph P. *Relationships of Chrysemyd Turtles of North America (Testudines: Emydidae).* Texas Tech University, Special Publications of the Museum No. 21. Lubbock: April 1984.

Wright, Albert Hazen, and Anna Allen Wright. *Handbook of Frogs and Toads of the United States and Canada.* Ithaca, New York: Comstock, 1949.

Index